D1462577

On the Tiger's Back

Leipzig, 1956. Voroshilov's visit. Ajao in procession as a Nigerian representative along with an Indian.

ON THE TIGER'S BACK

Aderogba Ajao

THE WORLD PUBLISHING COMPANY

CLEVELAND AND NEW YORK

Published by *The World Publishing Company*
2231 West 110th Street, Cleveland 2, Ohio

Library of Congress Catalog Card Number: 62–15705

FIRST EDITION

GBWP

CONTENTS

When I stepped out of the aircraft at Ikeja Airport, Lagos, I felt as a drowning man is supposed to feel. I had not seen my country for seven years, and I thought it might be looking at me just as much as I was looking at it. When I left Nigeria I was seeking for something, seeking a set of ideas, a magic formula. I remembered all this. I remembered my discovery of the existence of a world beyond Nigeria. I remembered the conflicts in my mind when I discovered how the British came to rule Nigeria. I remembered my time of study in Britain and the things I learnt there—some true and some false, as I afterwards discovered—from friends and enemies. And I remembered my seven years in Eastern Germany to which partly attraction, partly enterprise, and partly conspiracy, had led me.

I had lost a number of illusions. Had my fellow countrymen picked some of them up in my absence?

THE LIMITS OF MY WORLD

CHAPTER 1

Lagos and the Universe

Only the sons of kings and serfs are never asked by their fathers, 'What are you going to be when you grow up?' Although my own father is a Yoruba Chief and a descendant of titled potentates in Oyo, a town north of Ibadan, capital of what is now the Western Region of Nigeria, the question was often put to me.

One day in 1946 my father summoned to his room my cousin and me, and put the familiar question to us.

This time my father seemed to accept my answer as an accomplished fact in a way he had not done before. I had always told him, and my friends, that my aim in life was to become a manufacturer. What I was going to manufacture varied with the years, but I had no doubt about the central idea. By 1946, in spite of my youth—I was sixteen—the only uncertainty was that I could not make up my mind between porcelain and glass.

Looking back, it seems to me that even as long ago as 1941 the desire to be a manufacturer and not a trader had been formed in my mind as a fairly powerful urge by watching the many traders waiting hour after hour inside our warehouse or on the doorstep and pavements outside our shop in Lagos. Some were sleeping, some half-awake, waiting for my uncle, or for my father, who would come in advance of a lorry loaded with various brands of imported English cigarettes.

The women waited to buy cigarettes or other imported goods and sometimes even after they had been waiting for long hours—ten hours was not unknown—they would have to be sent away because the European mercantile houses with which my father dealt were unable to supply them. But as sure as daylight the women would be back next day to wait, or to get what they wanted.

This was a war year. At least everybody said that a world war was on. Our masters, the Government of the United Kingdom, were at war and it seemed to follow automatically that Nigeria too was at war with Germany. It was during the war that one of those minor changes took place which to a boy are vivid and striking. Until about 1943 it was to my parents I looked for an explanation of all phenomena. It was with pride and satisfaction that I discovered that our roles were being reversed, and that more and more often I was being asked to read the English newspapers to my elders when they wanted to hear the latest war news.

Lagos, an island city, which lies within the seaboard creeks of the Bight of Benin, is a crowded, lively place, with marked strains of the various elements in its complex history, both African and European. Through it the products of the hinterland, whether they were casks of palm oil or cocoa beans or slaves, went to the sea and into it came the missionary and the trader (hand in hand as it seemed to some) with the Bible and the gin bottle, and the trading beads and the guns and the splendid principles of democratic government.

Through all the changes, up to the period when British administration reached its pervasive maximum, the social fabric of the Yoruba people remained not, it is true, intact, but very nearly so, an old and cherished set of relationships, a pattern of custom which had been carefully preserved and went on in its own way.

My father was the second of my grandfather's three sons. His elder brother—'senior' brother is the word we use in English—was a qualified chemist and pharmacist, but my father had not been sent to school in the 'Western' sense. In 1914 when he was just sixteen years old he left Awe-Oyo, the traditional place of residence of the family—the family seat, if you like—and came to Lagos. He began trading there with a capital of six shillings, which represented his total material assets. It was while he was engaged in this trade, which very soon began to operate on a much larger scale, that I grew up beside him. The market women called him 'Baba Egba', which means roughly 'President' or 'Oga', an address of honour. His younger brother ('junior' is our word) whom he had helped to educate, became his closest confidant. I was always impressed by the way these two men were able to work together although their temperaments were poles apart. My uncle did all the clerical work, kept the books, wrote the letters, calculated profit and loss. My father made the decisions and supervised the day-to-day work of the business.

The family had many dependants, for it is the custom of the Yoruba people, as it is of many other African societies, to take responsibility for a wide cousinship.

By the time I became actively aware of my surroundings my father had been living for over a quarter of a century in the largely detribalized atmosphere of the metropolitan capital, but our house, or rather group of houses in Lagos, reproduced the essentials of a typical Yoruba compound.

These dependants naturally have an interest in maintaining the prestige of the family which nourishes them, and so it was from them as well as from my father, uncles and immediate cousins that I got to know about my ancestors and about my people.

My father felt so strongly about their place of origin that my mother was sent back to the old family house in Awe in the early part of 1930, expressly so that I could first see the light of day in that place, which I chose to do on May 12th. The matter was not merely one of sentiment for, if my mother had not spent the later period of her pregnancy in Awe, and I had not been born in the town, according to the tradition of my people, I would be known as Jara Awe, that is, a citizen by right of parentage, which would have meant that I should have carried less weight at any of the town's meetings or festivals than someone who was Omo Awe, a citizen by right of birth.

I was brought to Lagos when I was only a few months old and did not visit Awe again until I was fourteen, whereas my father made at least a yearly pilgrimage, but my status was, in principle, unimpaired. There were daily reminders when I was a boy of the greatness that our family once held in Yoruba society.

Two themes were drummed into my head as a boy: the glorious future of Africa and a firm faith that nothing in this world is unattainable if one is determined, righteous, well-mannered and, above all, respectful to one's elders.

My father has always and often told how grateful he was to his mother. When he was still a boy his father died and his mother died also before he was a full-grown man. My father used to tell us how his mother had made him count cowrie shells, which were then used as currency, over and over again. At that time he regarded it as a punishment but later on, when his own business began to grow in Lagos, he came to believe that his determination had somehow been steeled by this exercise.

I came to recognize that my father's strict code of conduct for us had been laid down in order to fit us to become responsible citizens. I must admit that some of my youthful impulses could not always be reconciled with this code of conduct and added to that was the usual conflict between the generations, and the effects of the difference in my own and my father's early surroundings.

This difference in early environment probably helped to create my mixed feelings about some of our family traditions. I was conscious of the bad effects of a narrow tribalism, even if only dimly at this stage. One of my ancestors, it appears, had been the Balogun of Awe, a title held now by my father—though almost entirely in an honorary capacity. In the old days the position was a cross between a local prime minister and military commander-in-chief. According to legend the present site of the town of Oyo was a gift to its people by the Balogun. And there is another tradition that the ruling house of Oyo provided the temporal head of the Yoruba people. My father is the Otun of Oyo.

Although I sensed the limitations of the tribal exclusiveness which all this implied, I had a strong sense of attachment to the people whom I knew in my daily life in Lagos, and could not detect any difference of feeling between myself and Kojo, the son of a Dahomian washman, or my neighbour Peter, whose parents came from Eastern Nigeria where tribes different from my own were dominant.

In my childhood, until I suppose I was about eight, I took it for granted that Lagos was the only place of human habitation. I assumed that all the people who inhabited the island must have been born there, a conclusion I drew from my instruction and from the Scriptures—my family was Christian—which said that God created only one man and one woman. The conclusion seemed to be confirmed by the legends of my own people, from which I learned that the universe contains seven worlds and that we could only pass from one to another when our spirits departed from our bodies, a process which could only take place when we were asleep or dead.

At this stage of my life, therefore, it did not strike me as odd that some of the inhabitants of Lagos who visited our shop had white skins. These people were referred to deferentially as 'Oga', meaning 'master', but since the same people addressed my father in this way also, I thought nothing of it. In 1939 I began to glimpse some doubts about the soundness of this view, for I learned that some Europeans had been separated off from everybody else and were being held in detention in King's College, a secondary school in Lagos. People began to talk about war. These Europeans were Germans.

It was thus that I became vaguely aware that Lagos society was not quite so monolithic as I had originally thought, and the discovery destroyed the ideal world in which I lived.

One of the aspects of the educational system under British rule, which may strike the observer as odd, was that I and my school fellows, apart from more utilitarian subjects, were given a grounding in Greek mythology and became familiar with the figures of the Greek pantheon. These stories fascinated many of us, partly I suppose because it was not difficult for us, familiar as we were with Yoruba legend, to accept the notion that superhuman beings with supernatural powers existed or had existed—it was much the same thing. And like the innumerable Yoruba stories, the Greek stories always had a lesson behind them. Although a more sophisticated view, developed later, might have led me to believe that the Greek stories had a somewhat different significance, as they were taught to us their cardinal message was that it pays to do good and to be loyal, to be courageous and faithful. And even more important in these legends appeared to be the idea that your sins would always catch up with you whatever you did.

When the realization that the world contained a great variety of people had been clearly fixed in my mind, I began to expand my mental horizons. By 1945 I had enough English vocabulary to be able to read the English newspapers tolerably well, and from the maps in those newspapers I learned rather more than I did from school geography lessons about the other countries and peoples of this planet.

Although I cannot have looked at it in this way in those days, I was at the crossroads of two patterns of thinking.

CHAPTER 2

Out

Class V of the Baptist Academy in Lagos contained pupils who were developing opinions which would probably have surprised the earnest missionaries who taught them. At that time the Baptist Academy was one of the few boys' secondary schools in Nigeria and there is no doubt about its quality. Many of Nigeria's leading men spent the formative part of their schooldays there.

After the Second World War, Nigerian schoolboys were beginning to feel the finger of destiny upon them. This is perhaps rather a high-flown way of putting it, but it reflects what our real feelings were. Our teachers would probably have been rather surprised at our interest in India's struggle for freedom, in the revolution in Indonesia, and in the Chinese Communist Party's struggle against Chiang kai-Shek and his American capitalist backers. I think we must have used these words—words like 'capitalist'—in their simple abusive sense because quite a number of us were members of what could only be called 'capitalist' families and had anything but a distaste for becoming rich ourselves.

I am not sure how it came about, but even when I was a schoolboy I had begun to be obsessed by an interest in technology and the need to apply it to Nigeria, as a condition of the successful outcome of the nationalist movement. I seem to have perceived, perhaps dimly and incoherently, that nationalist fervour of a purely political kind, although all very right and proper in its own way, was going to be valueless unless it brought about the industrialization of my country.

Even as a schoolboy in a respectable missionary school, which taught nothing that the British interest could possibly disapprove of, the notion that Nigeria and other colonies were 'exploited' by the British was firmly embedded in my mind. And when I began to think about these things I found no difficulty in believing that

16

Britain was careful to prevent the industrial development of Nigeria in order to extract the country's raw materials profitably and to frustrate the emergence of a possible industrial competitor. These conceptions were commonplace in the nationalist movement and were accepted by active-minded schoolboys because they fitted in well with our emotional attitudes, and because the factual correctives were absent.

My schoolfellows and I darted about like little fish in our pursuit of political ideas, and although I daresay we were very ill-informed and, in this often forgotten and neglected part of West Africa, got our facts completely wrong, the pattern of our ideas was clear enough and not nearly so incoherent as the words we used might lead one to suppose.

We were all nationalists and wished our country to be free of foreign rule. But even in our small society we reflected the varieties of opinion that marked the thinking of our elders. Some of us were all fire and said, 'Out with the imperialists. Let us not be diverted from this by tedious questions about the country's viability.' Others said, 'Let us fix now a date for independence, say in five or ten years. That will give us plenty of time to discuss those trifling technical details.' Others said, 'Yes, independence for Nigeria, but surely no one can seriously suggest that it will be possible within the next twenty-five years'.

At this time I was reading everything I could lay my hands on and was growing more and more interested in accounts of countries which had become rapidly industrialized. At that time I could see only the differences between success and failure and had no time for moral reflections about means and ends.

In my family we began to talk about what was going to happen to me when I left the Baptist Academy. A lot of the discussion took place out of my hearing because decisions of this kind, in Yoruba circles, were not thought to need the counsel of young persons. But I wanted to go abroad and my father, although he himself had no such experience, seemed to accept the idea that it was the thing to do.

At that time the Nigerian Government, which was, of course, in all decisive things in the hands of the British administrators, took a good deal of interest in helping Nigerians to go to the United Kingdom for further education. There was a constant stream of Nigerians on their way to England in search of the degrees and diplomas that would make their fortune, increase the status of their families and help in the development of their country. There were some who went elsewhere, to the United States, and—though rarer, mainly because of language difficulties—to other European countries or to the Middle East.

In my case financial assistance or scholarships did not arise so that there was no need to bring the government into it. But, as I recall what went on in my own mind, a good deal of our ultimate decision that I should act independently arose from the fact that I believed that nothing the government did for anybody was any good at all. Government help was the kiss of death. The evidence on which I based this belief was probably non-existent, but there it was and as far as I was concerned all those earnest officials who were doing their best were getting no credit for it.

We had a copy of the latest edition of the *Public Schools Year Book* and it was carefully combed for the best school for me to attend. George Watson's College, Edinburgh, was the one we finally chose. The reasons were various but they all seemed to add up to what we wanted. First of all the very fact that it was in Scotland, a country that had once been independent of England, was an attraction in itself, and many well-known Nigerians, particularly doctors, had been trained at Edinburgh University. And George Watson's was a Merchant Company school, and, of course, my own family were merchants too. And then the Board of Governors included a reassuringly large number of knights. And its reputation seemed otherwise sound.

I sailed for Liverpool in the Elder Dempster mail-boat *Apapa* in April 1948. I was not the only Nigerian on his way to find the golden apple, but I was one of the youngest, although not particularly disconcerted by the fact.

At Liverpool docks my entry was easy, smooth, politely conducted. For all the anti-imperialist sentiments with which my mind had been filled, there was all the same an image of Britain and British society which gave both the highest qualities. The notion was firmly embedded that things we did badly in Nigeria were done perfectly in England. We accepted the idea that Britain was rich and powerful, and had organized itself in such a way that little things did not go wrong. Officials knew their business and would be just in their decisions which would be made quickly. Indeed the image was so strongly implanted that in some ways it did Britain more harm than good. The imagined standard was so high that the smallest failure to match up to it had a disproportionate effect.

This was why my smooth and politely conducted passage through immigration and customs, where there was no question about my right of entry, no vexatious questions about my documents, no rudeness, no delays, all of which impressed me, but was no less than I expected, was almost immediately erased by an encounter so trivial that it should have had no effect.

Before joining the train that was to take me to Edinburgh, I wanted a cup of tea. In the docks I saw a stall. A large blowzy young woman was pouring cups of tea out of a tea-boiler, rattling cups and saucers, pushing sugar bowls and milk jugs about on her swill-spattered counter. A lot of men wanted cups of tea, and wanted them in a hurry. There was a certain amount of amiable pushing and shoving, and loud interchanges over the counter. My ear was not in tune with what was being said, and perhaps the woman did not understand my speech.

'Well, what you want? Haven't all day to wait for you t'make up your mind. Got me work to do. Don't stand there gaping.'

No more than that. But I was being shouted at. The place was scruffy, although there was nothing wrong with the tea when I got it, and it was cheap. It was a dock workers' tea stall, not a tea-room. But it did not square with my ideas of what was to be expected in England. It wasn't part of the image. And long after I had realized the simple reality, and the harmlessness of the episode, I still felt the shock.

I arrived by train in Edinburgh on the evening of the day I had disembarked in Liverpool. I had the address of the Colonial Students' Hostel, Palmerston Road. I was expected. My name was on their lists. The manageress was a West Indian, and the rest of the occupants were all 'colonials', a word of wide meaning. There were other Africans, West Indians, a few Asians, including Indians and Pakistanis.

I shared a room with a Nigerian and another African. Most of the rooms accommodated two or three students, and of course there were sitting-rooms and a dining-room. There had been correspondence with a firm of Edinburgh solicitors, picked out of a directory, like the school. They were to act as guardians, and look after my money. But they handed over all my money to me the first time I called on them and although they dealt fairly with me, the eye they kept on me was remote and cool.

And the next day or on the day after I presented myself at George Watson's College. This was quite a long time ago, and I cannot pretend, like a novelist, to remember details. A great deal has become cloudy, especially about the school itself. But it was a friendly place, and the boys, middle-class boys from prosperous professional or mercantile Scottish families, without exception that I can remember, treated me with interest and kindliness. They did nothing to make me feel that the fact that I was an African put me at a disadvantage or was any reason for them to criticize or disapprove of me. Some of them asked me to their homes. I liked them, and seeing them—it did not happen regularly or in total very often—in their own environment made me want to lodge with a Scottish family and leave the Colonial Hostel, which was all right in its way but because its occupants were all 'colonials' too, it seemed to me to have nothing to do with the country in which I was living.

Although I had enrolled in George Watson's as a result of private enterprise my registration with the Colonial Hostel authorities had, of course, been arranged officially, and there was a student adviser who was supposed to be available to help students who got into difficulties or who wanted advice. It was him I asked to arrange for my transfer to a private family. It took time, I was told. It was not easy to find the right kind of family. It never came about, although I pressed for it again and again.

I had been welcomed by the Headmaster on my arrival at the school. I liked him. He made me feel welcome and when he said that I should never hesitate to approach him about any problem I encountered, I was given confidence that powerful help was at my disposal.

I was a day-boy, coming to school in the morning with the rest of the day pupils and leaving with them in the evening. The rest to their homes, myself to the Colonial Students' Hostel. In my class we studied English literature, history, including contemporary history, mathematics, French, science, which meant physics and chemistry. In Nigeria English meant English language primarily, since English was to us a second language, but in Scotland at that stage of schooling, the emphasis was on literature rather than on language. It was the current events part of the history that interested me most. I seemed to be more interested in world affairs than my school-fellows, although I may have imagined this. I felt that political developments affected me more than they did them. I was more deeply involved in them somehow. Their society was stable, largely satisfied. Their country, although I knew Scotland was ready to say that it was a poor country, was industrialized: it had been through the process. My country was different. It was on the edge of new things, it wanted changes and what was in the past was of no value now.

I had no complaint with the school. It was a good, even an excellent school. But I was dissatisfied. Where was it getting me? There must be some short-cut to what I wanted, instead of this ploughing on, the perpetual schoolboy, when there was so much of practical value to learn for which academic acquirements were of little value in the broad sense and no use at all to a Nigerian.

What I heard in the hostel rapidly confirmed me in these notions, and in fact must have had a good deal to do with their creation. The hostel was a wonderful place for talking. We had not much else to do, a good deal of the time, because there was little money to spare for artificial amusements. So we talked, and we talked, as colonials to colonials, in isolation from our surroundings, and every grievance or fancied slight that we encountered was worried over again and again like a dog with a bone it had buried and dug up to chew over, and buried again.

While the others played table-tennis, or tried to study through the clip of the ping-pong balls and the rattle of voices, we sat and talked, and talked, and talked. I was the only schoolboy in the hostel. The others were at Edinburgh University or at technical colleges.

One of the talkers was a fellow Nigerian, Yemi Ayadeji, who was taking an Arts degree at the University, and was a very active member of the Students' Union. He was a natural oppositionist, a rebel, suspicious of authority, sceptical of all motives and fluently persuasive. I suppose Ayadeji had a good deal of influence on me, although I imagined I was making up my mind about things unaided. Although he was taking an Arts course, Ayadeji was very strong on the subject of Nigeria's need to develop industrially, and he continually impressed on me that I was wasting my time in Edinburgh.

Our talk was full of the wickedness of imperialism and colonialism. 'These British', he said, 'will never let go. Once an imperialist always an imperialist. We have to fight them. Do you think a country like Britain that has built itself up into a rich capitalist state is going to let go its possessions unless it is forced to. Don't be a fool. They dare not let go. This rotten capitalist society is bound to fall, but we have to help it to fall by giving it a hard push.' There was a good deal of strong language, a lot of hot air, no doubt, but it was lively and stimulating.

At that time there was no question of Communism. Marxist notions, as such, really didn't enter into the matter. There was a language of political opposition, broadly left-wing, which was common to all. It became clear to me later that there was more than coincidence in the identity of the Communist line and that of our form of nationalism, and I have no doubt that Ayadeji was a Communist. But whether he was or not does not seem to have mattered. It was beside the point.

Nationalists could only be nationalists if they were opposed to something. Nationalism, for the people of dependencies, is a positive thing, but it has no guts unless its strongest emotions are those against its overlords. That is why outside observers think nationalist fervour shows an indifference to what is important, meaning the viability of the country concerned; and concentrates far too much on polemic against 'imperialists' and other sometimes mythical enemies. But the fact remains that it is anger that is the first and indispensable ingredient of a nationalist movement. Without it, nothing can be generated.

Communism, as I say, did not come into the matter at this stage of my thinking. I knew about it, in a vague way, and it must have filtered into my mind that the only people who seemed to have the right ideas about the imperialists were the Communists. They had the right slogans, anyway, and they claimed to have a scientific certainty about the solution of political and economic problems.

My dissatisfactions with my progress in Edinburgh grew rapidly to a critical point. I had to go. I had to get a technical training. I wanted to know how to run a business, how to buy and sell, how to make money: and English literature and history scarcely seemed the right way to go about it.

I suppose I did not behave very well about all this, and it worried me. How could I explain to my family in Lagos what I wanted to do and why? If I involved myself in lengthy correspondence with them, I would waste time, get nowhere. Better to take the plunge, enrol myself somewhere else, somewhere right this time, and present them with the event after it had taken place. I wrote to the College of Commerce and Technology in Leicester, was accepted, and packed my bags and left Edinburgh.

CHAPTER 3

Into the Net

_____

When I went to Leicester I was beginning to feel my manhood strong upon me. I had seen life, I had heard new ideas. I was no longer the schoolboy from Lagos, who knew nothing. I knew something about life, and I had shed illusions. And I thought I knew what I wanted. There was still my obsession about technical training, technical wisdom, which would give me the secret of fortune and at the same time enable me to help my country to shake off foreign rule and bring itself out into the world, into a world in which it would not survive without industrialization.

Looking back, I can see that I had a pretty naïve set of notions, but the central proposition was not wrong. It wasn't wrong then and it isn't wrong now. But I probably thought the whole thing was easy, if only I could find out the secret.

One of the courses I took at Leicester was on economics. I thought that economics was the study of economic and industrial development. I expected to learn how to run an industry, how to run a business, how to assess the swing of prices, how, in other words, to be successful and make money. Economic theory, the economic classics, was not what I really wanted. I remember in one lecture hearing a long disquisition about the fluctuations of markets, including stock market values. I asked the lecturer a question: 'I have heard your lecture with interest, but why have you not told us how to predict these fluctuations? What is the use of learning the theory of these matters if it cannot be used to predict events?' The class laughed at me, and the lecturer explained that however sound economic theories, there were imponderables in so many aspects of the business that prediction could not be accurate and it was better not to indulge in it.

I could see that I had expected too much, but the point rankled. Surely there must be some practical way of treating these matters in a purely materialistic way, and getting a workable answer.

In Leicester I stayed in one of the Halls of Residence. This was much more satisfactory than the hostel in Edinburgh, because here there was no question of being tucked away in a polite sort of colonial ghetto, cut off from the rest of humanity. The mixture was complete. There were Africans and Asians and Arabs and West Indians, as there had been in Edinburgh, but there were also English, Welsh, Scots and all the rest of them. I was glad I had changed horses, and was prepared to work and to enjoy myself.

It was only after I had lived and tried to study in Eastern Europe under a Communist régime that I realized how sharp is the contrast between a country, like Britain, where no authority even suggests that a student should interest himself in politics, and a Communist country where an interest in politics is inescapable, obligatory, even if it is in a political theory and practice of a particular type to the exclusion of all others.

I was interested in politics in Leicester because I wanted to be, because I *was* deeply interested, because it was part of my need in life, an essential part of my nourishment as a human being. There were plenty of students who were not interested in politics in Leicester, who wanted no part of it. But to me, politics, and talk about political issues, were essentials, and anyone who wanted to talk politics would find no difficulty in getting me to join in.

As a lonely student, with no particular ties, I naturally looked round various student organizations in order to see which would suit me best. All the political parties were organized, except that I think the Communist Party which had once been organized within the college had been kicked out or had faded out.

The Labour Party was in power in Britain at that time. It now strikes me as strange that with all my curiosity about politics, with my natural instinct for the Left because the Right, in relation to Nigeria, could not possibly have drawn me to it, I was never for a moment attracted to the British Labour Party. I read about it, of course, and heard people talk about it, but never for a moment did it have the slightest appeal for me. I accepted the idea, which was universally accepted, within my acquaintance by colonial students, that Labour Party policies for the colonies were, for all practical purposes, the same as those of the Conservative Party. If they said otherwise, they did not mean it. If they meant otherwise, the 'imperialists' would prevent them putting their policies into effect. I recognize that this was all very unfair to the Labour Party, but the fact remains that it never managed to appeal to us.

My absorption in politics grew, and I have no doubt did my college studies little good. I read everything; I haunted the Leicester Public Library when I should no doubt have been haunting the college library. I read fat books about the industrial development of the United States, of Japan, of the Soviet Union. I read about Hitler's rise to power. Who had the secret? Was it Hitler, perhaps? Maybe he had been right in many ways about the economy of Germany, and went astray and was destroyed for the wrong reasons. What lessons could I learn from all this for myself and for Nigeria? I was biting off a good deal more than I could chew, but fortunately did not know it.

I had not been many months in Leicester when my political awakening began to take on a more recognizable pattern. My reading had included Edgar Snow's *Red Star Over China*, a book beyond measure exciting, and available in the Leicester Public Library, but not in the college library. There was the *Daily Worker* which seemed to be saying all the right things about the colonies writhing under the heel of the imperialists. I read, and I talked. And I got more pleasure from talking to people who agreed with me than with those who didn't.

It was in this way that I first came across the Young Communist League. Looking back on these earnest young people after my life under the disciplines of a Communist State, I can see how lightly indoctrinated they were. There was dogmatism, and a faith in the ultimate rightness of the Marxist-Leninist-Stalinist thesis, but there was a willingness to admit the existence (although not the ultimate validity) of other ideas in a way which was quite out of the question for their contemporaries in Eastern Europe.

Apart from the sympathy I had for their point of view there was also the fact that the Young Communists were very friendly to me, and seemed to take my African-ness in their stride. They never laughed at my ideas about the regeneration of the world and the advancement of the peoples of Africa as others sometimes did in a rough and ready, but seldom malicious, way. I made friends with them. I went to their houses.

They seemed to have the right ideas, and above all they had a kind of certainty about the rightness, and the ultimate victory of their point of view, which was exactly what I sought. In the welter of ideas which prevail in an intellectually unrestricted society, it is probably seldom realized how very disconcerting and unsatisfying the apparent absence of fixed political theories can be. A seeker after political foundations, in British society, is like a child whose parents take to extremes the notion that a child is not to be frustrated and must never be compelled to do what he does not want to do. Such a child is often unhappy, and uncertain, with nothing firm to cling to, nothing to save him from ceaseless uncertainty.

This notion was one of the factors which led me towards Communism: certainty. It was immensely attractive, and many a time, in the countless discussions in which I took part during this period, privately, with individuals, or later, in the more organized occasions arranged by the Young Communist League, my own doubts were swamped by the Communist argument that even if certain phenomena did not seem to fit into the prescribed pattern that was only because one saw them from the wrong angle, through the distorting lens of bourgeois thinking, or because, unhappy wretch that I was, I had been brought up under alien domination.

And there was Jean. Jean was about eighteen. She worked in an office. And she was treasurer of one of the Leicester groups of the Young Communist League. Jean was a nice friendly sort of girl who liked talking about politics, and she devoted her young fervours to Marxism-Leninism in much the same way as some of her less intelligent contemporaries devoted theirs to clothes or dancing.

There were quite a lot of people like Jean about in Leicester and I suppose also in other towns of the same sort in England. However deluded they may have been about the Soviet Union's domestic history or about its intentions towards the non-Communist world, these young people were probably sincerely attached to certain perfectly respectable ideals. They believed that the world could be improved and that it was worth making an effort to improve it. And, what is more, they felt it their duty to make the effort themselves. They got pleasure from the conviction that the society in which they lived was a bad one and that there were abuses that could be removed. And in post-war British society there were many things that needed attention. Parliamentary democracy in Britain failed to appeal to young people who were in general among the 'have nots' and when the Communist Party told them firmly that the solution was easy and was one that they could help to work out, there was no reason why they should not believe it.

The main trouble with foreign students in England at that time was that there was not enough for them to do, and they had not enough money for the kind of amusements such as Leicester offered, like picture-houses, or pubs. So the Students' Club or the coffee houses became their meeting ground and their endless hours were spent on talk.

There was one Leicester club in particular where we used to meet. It was an international club set up mainly for students by some philanthropic body with no political attitudes, but it was, in fact, the place where political ideas were discussed at length and where sundry plots were hatched. It always amused me to think that the kindly sponsors of the club probably believed that its existence kept students' minds off mischievous political notions when in fact—what with the unreadable books provided and our inability to devote our whole time to playing table-tennis—we expended all our surplus energy in trying to bring about the doom of the imperialists, colonialists and capitalists in whose world, although not exactly in whose bosom, we were living.

The master-mind of the group was an Iraqi student who was eventually sent away from England by his own government whose patience with his ability to create trouble and to get mixed up in what seemed to them undesirable political activities became exhausted. Salek was one of those dynamic characters with an enormous amount of energy and an endless flow of argument against all the Communist targets. When he was launched on a diatribe against British imperialism in the Middle East, or the terrible miseries of the capitalist system, nothing could stop him, and his eloquence was very persuasive. But Salek was no mere talker: he had all sorts of ideas about political action and he had his eye on the future.

Not far from Leicester there was a military training establishment, at Loughborough. Among the trainees there were some Pakistanis. It was Salek's idea that we should get in touch with those Pakistanis when they came to Leicester to taste its social joys. It was not so much that he wanted to subvert them or to induce them to blow up their training establishment. He simply wanted to identify them, make himself known to them on the assumpton that people trained in this way might return to Pakistan and eventually occupy positions in the Pakistan Army of comparative power. The time might come, if a revolutionary situation developed in Iraq, when the contact could be usefully renewed.

It sounds fantastic now. But was it so fantastic? There have been military *coups d'état* in both Iraq and Pakistan and one of them was accomplished by officers who got some if not all of their inspiration, not to speak of active aid, from the Communists.

As a member of the Young Communist League in Leicester I attended many of their meetings and drank their coffee as the gatherings moved from house to house. These meetings varied. Sometimes there were members only: sometimes the members brought friends. When the formal talks ended the discussions which followed would take for granted fewer Communist propositions and encouraged an attitude of sweet reasonableness, permitting the holding of diverse views. It was by these means that the Young Communist League kept up its numbers because there was a certain amount of wastage in the membership. Young men and women drifted in and out, drifting out if they were only half-in intellectually when they found something more amusing to do or perhaps when they got a higher wage.

Occasionally some of us got involved with local politics when we helped candidates seeking election to municipal councils. These candidates were not necessarily Communists but could belong to any part of the Left of centre, preferably as Left as possible. I do not remember that we ever succeeded in getting any of our candidates in but it merely convinced us of the rightness of our cause, and the blindness, stupidity, and wickedness of everybody else. We knew, and we were happy in the knowledge, that a great cause demands its martyrs and that we were in the vanguard of a heroic struggle against the Titans.

I lived for about a year in the hostel at Leicester. It was a reconditioned nineteenth-century villa, so I was told, and had to take the fact on trust since I had no particular eye for the finer points of architecture. It was big, anyway, and it stood in Glenfield Road on the outskirts of the town. There were about a dozen students off and on, for they came and went.

When I try to recall exactly who they were and in what proportion of nationalities, I find that my arithmetic never quite works out. I suppose that those who made the deepest impression on me may only have seemed to be there all the time, and those I never particularly noticed were there all the time.

The place was well run, with rules only stringent enough to keep it in working order. All the students came from my college. There was a housekeeper who managed the place, and there were cleaners. Most of us had to share a room, but there was plenty of space, considering everything, and after all students have no special claim to live in luxurious conditions. There was a lounge, I remember, with leather armchairs. We all had breakfast in the hostel, but not a midday meal. This we had at college, or in a café somewhere, or we had none. And we had supper, or dinner, or whatever it was called, again at the hostel. The meals weren't bad, although at the price we paid (£2 to £3 a week) they were not very exciting. Good and plain, and the foreigners had to accept that they were on an English diet and there was not much they could do about it. We could not afford to pay for the hostel and eat meals out as well.

There was a real attempt to make the hostel work smoothly. We had our meals at separate tables, or at any rate not at one big central table, so that we could choose our companions if we wanted to. And the place was clean. Altogether, there wasn't much to complain about in the purely material sense, in the villa in Glenfield Road. The dissatisfaction and boredom, and the search for escape and inspiration were not a direct outcome of either unsympathetic or physically uncomfortable surroundings, and it is difficult to see what else could have been done, except perhaps to show some realization that a collection of students from countries in political ferment, or about to be, would find some sort of outlet somewhere. I suppose that in a country like England, the notion of leaving people to find their own salvation without any attempt to direct them is too ingrained to change. But it produces some funny results. I have often wondered about this, this English *knowing* what works (giving them the benefit of the doubt for the moment) but thinking it is self-evident and not worth the bother

Into the Net

of explaining or of persuading other people to adopt it. But I must not start wondering about it now.

Of the ten or a dozen students there at various times, I recall that there were usually between three and five English or Scottish or Welsh natives. There were two Nigerians, of whom I was one. My fellow Nigerian was from Lagos, and had a scholarship. He sniffed around political matters like a dog afraid of getting bitten. There was one Cameroonian. The main thing I remember about him was that he was always complaining about the cold. He was a Civil Servant who had come to England to get a qualification which would give him a step up in the administration. He was not what could fairly be called politically simple, but I think the Civil Servant part of him was on the top, and he had no wish to involve himself in the discussion of large political ideas or their possible effects. There were six Iraqis, one Israeli (that is, then, a Palestinian), one Eurasian Malay and one Indian.

My room-mate for some time was an English grammar-school-boy. Atkins was his name. He was perfectly amiable, but I could never get a spark of politics out of him. He was in fact a conventional standard-pattern English student, who wanted to get on with his studies, and who obviously thought that an interest in politics was all very well for a lot of slightly dubious foreigners, who couldn't be expected to know about these things by instinct and therefore had to be arguing about them all the time instead of getting on with their education.

In the hostel, in the evenings, we used to find ourselves trying to fill up the gap between dinner and bedtime. Often the atmosphere, for those of us who were far away from home, was dull to a painful degree. We should have been studying, no doubt, but we preferred to talk. In situations like that there is always someone who takes the lead. Usually it was the Iraqi. He was an urbanized middle-class type—it would have been difficult for him to get to England to study if his family had not had means. He regarded himself as a genuine Marxist, but an impure one.

Heresy, so intolerable to the true Stalinist of the period, was widespread among foreign students, and among the indigenous variety in Britain too—that one could be a Communist with reservations, a Communist with national prejudices, a Communist who was prepared to see some good in some of the things that went on in hopelessly un-Marxist countries like Britain.

31

What really made Salek tick was anti-imperialism, which for him meant outside influence on Iraq and other Middle East countries where Western Europeans had an interest and expressed it by various forms of control and interference. It was against British influence that Salek came out strongest. At the same time, he admired England for many things. I often met with this sort of thing, and certainly could have watched it going on in my own mind.

It is perfectly possible to admire a country and its people and its institutions, and at the same time to hate it passionately, to wish for its destruction, to wish to see its self-satisfied smile wiped off its fat red face. I have heard all kinds of fancy attempts, by anthropologists and political and social analysts, to explain this double attitude, to go into it as if it was something mysterious and inexplicable. To my mind there is nothing particularly mysterious about it. What else could be expected? The English should be familiar with it, if anyone should be. The class structure in England is really very like the relationship between foreign rulers and dependent peoples. Many Nigerians read the writings of H. G. Wells, who depicted very well certain kinds of social resentment. Whenever that social resentment becomes even slightly sophisticated, which is probably just as soon as the idea is generated that human relations are not permanent and can be changed, what was formerly acquiescent, and even in some cases genuine gratitude to the superior being, gives place to the desire for radical change and a deep dislike of the benefactor.

Britain occupies a curious position in all this. The very indifference to criticism—especially from foreign students—preserved a kind of reluctant respect. There is respect too, for the British system of giving living space and education to thousands of foreign students and at the same time leaving them to their own devices when it could be influencing their political attitudes. It is one of the ironies of history that so many revolutionaries should have learnt their philosophies in the countries whose interests they set out to destroy. The Indonesians who were to form the new republic after the war learned their liberal and 'progressive' ideas in the universities of the Netherlands. The Indo-Chinese learned theirs at the Sorbonne or in the cafés with Thorez. The Indians and West Africans licked their political ice-cream in the London School of Economics and, somehow, in the Inns of Court.

THROUGH THE BARRIER

C

CHAPTER 4

The Deal in Hamburg

In the autumn of 1950 I left Leicester and returned to Lagos. I had not succeeded in doing what I set out to do. I had obtained no academic or technical qualification, at least on paper. I consoled myself with the thought that I was a good deal wiser than when I had left Nigeria. I had shed illusions, I had made a lot of friends and acquaintances among those who understood the nature of politics. No longer was I simply a colonial student, but a politically-conscious African nationalist with some knowledge of Communist theory and revolutionary practice—although that practice was for the most part with my tongue alone. When I got back to Lagos I had to restore my credit by returning to my father's business.

My zeal, and my belief that I was properly equipped by knowledge and experience, led me to carry on a small import company of my own. This had its ups and downs, which have no part in the main thread of my story, but it was in the pursuit of an elusive success in business that early in 1952 I again left Nigeria for Europe. I had prospects of obtaining a consignment of cement from Eastern Europe at a favourable price. This took me to Hamburg. In the Hotel Vierjahreszeiten I met two friendly men who introduced themselves as representatives of the cement company. We got on very well. We chatted about the world economic situation, about business prospects, about developments in Africa.

I was highly pleased with the encounter for it held out a promise that I would be able to complete a satisfactory deal and return to Lagos with something very like the golden apple in my pocket. As my journey had been planned, I had to go to Norway in pursuit of some other trading prospect, but my friends at the Vierjahreszeiten were most insistent that I should hurry back and rejoin them in Berlin to complete the cement contract. I had meant to go to Paris from Norway, but my friends were so pressing that I cancelled the visit. My accumulated wisdom about humanity did not then enable me to see that everything was a little too smooth.

My two friends were all courtesy, and came to meet me at the frontier. It was most fortunate that they were there because I ran into visa difficulties. I had not paid much attention to the need for special permits. I must have thought that because I was an African, the authorities would take an easy view or would quickly appreciate that I was a sympathizer with Communism and not the sort of person who should be annoyed by bureaucratic treatment at frontier posts. I did not have to resolve this philosophical problem because my two friends offered to go ahead and clear the matter up.

A train left every hour for Berlin. My friends were to telephone back to the frontier post when they had fixed everything so that I could catch an early train to the capital where I would be met. It did not occur to me that it was rather odd that two 'businessmen' who were, presumably, trading for a profit should have such ready influence with the East German immigration authorities.

Before they left for Berlin we had joined a group of people at the frontier post who were to keep me company while waiting. After we had talked about this and that for a while, I was informed that it was going to take a little longer to arrange things but that my new friends could find me a roof for the night. I was, in fact, taken by car to a Russian military camp near Magdeburg about 50 miles inside the East German frontier.

I was tired. There was nothing to argue about, and I was not disposed to ask too many questions. This was the point of no return as it turned out. If I had told them I had changed my mind, and didn't want any cement any more, and wanted to go to Paris after all, I do not think I would have succeeded in changing my direction.

The next morning I was visited by a stranger, a civilian, who called himself 'George' and who turned up several times in the future. He was very apologetic about all the delay and changes of plan and hoped that I had not been inconvenienced by any of their clumsy but well-intentioned efforts to make me comfortable. He told me that to make up for the delay, I would be able to go direct from Magdeburg to Potsdam.

The car was large and powerful. The curtains were drawn on the partition between us and the driver's compartment as well as on the side and back windows. I was feeling very uneasy by this time.

'Why are the curtains drawn?'

'Ah, that. It is nothing, it is merely the custom.'

I was in no position to argue about what were or were not the customs of the country. I did not feel disposed to continue the discussion. The journey was silent for the most part. I had two companions, who did not bother very much to keep up a flow of idle chatter. Their task was completed and it would be for others to carry on the next stage. Our destination was a villa in Potsdam. There was a suite of rooms for me; I was invited to wash and shave. It was supposed that I was tired after my long journey. I *was* tired, but whether it was mostly my mental journey that was affecting me or the physical one is hard to say.

I undressed and bathed. Back in the bedroom I found, over a chair, a pair of pyjamas and a dressing-gown, not my own. All my clothes, my brief case, my passport, my return ticket, my personal papers and everything else I had with me, had disappeared. There was an electric push-button bell in the room. I pressed it rather gingerly, expecting the whole building to fall down about my ears.

A Russian in uniform came in with a question mark on his face.

'Where are my clothes?'

'Niet ponemaja.'

'Where is my passport?'

'Niet ponemaja.'

'Where is my brief case?'

'Niet ponemaja.'

I heard this 'I do not understand' many times thereafter. This time it sounded like the shutting of a prison door.

I sat in my new pyjamas and dressing-gown and looked for a long time at the wall in front of me. I did not see the material objects round me very clearly for some time, but when I did I noticed for the first time that the doors leading out of the suite had keyholes but no handles, and the windows had only a small opening, high up.

For eight days I had no visitors. I was fed well and regularly, but I was saved from a breakdown of my nerves by being provided with twenty English cigarettes a day. Somehow these cigarettes were a lifeline to ordinary humanity. I knew perfectly well that the supplying of them was no more than routine and was meant to balance the serious misgivings that I was bound to feel by being virtually locked up and incommunicado, but I could not help pretending to myself that I owed the cigarettes to some kindly individual somewhere along the line of authority who wished me well.

There were books in plenty, I discovered later, in another part of the villa, and these I had endless time to read. Dickens was there, Thackeray, Tolstoy, Voltaire, Lermontov and many others in English, French and German. I borrowed many of them and turned the pages of many of them, but I must say I do not remember much of what I read.

My state of mind at this time is in many ways the key to what happened subsequently. I had been for all practical purposes kidnapped. I had been enticed by a simple ruse—my interest in a cement contract—and had fallen for it easily and quickly. I had even presented myself at the East German frontier asking 'to be taken care of'. In the villa the whole thing came out into the open.

But it was not quite as simple as that. I knew I was in the hands of the Russians. But while I deeply resented having been tricked and felt very alone and very alarmed in a vague way about what might happen to me, it must be remembered that I had a great admiration for the Russians. My whole attitude was conditioned by what I had been told about them by my Communist friends, but it was rather like suddenly finding myself in the hands of minor attendants of the Olympian gods—persons basically benevolent, and, of course, exalted, but apt to be rather chancy and Olympian in their actions. I was certainly still at the stage of thinking that if by my rather humble standards, kidnapping and holding a man against his will was objectionable, the same acts by the Russians had a different character. They might be nerve-racking and worrying for me, but as a Communist sympathizer who was quite prepared to admit that he was one, their ultimate intentions towards me could only be good.

And there was this to it, too. Up to now my life plans had somehow failed to fulfil themselves. I had spent years in the United Kingdom without getting very far, and the spectacular success in business which I was frantically seeking had not materialized. I had enjoyed the intellectual excitement of my membership of the Communist Party and the dreamworld of the perfect Soviet society. So that when I found myself actually in Russian hands, I was in a way flattered that they should take so much trouble over me. At that time, too, there was an element of relief. I would no longer be responsible for my own fate or for past mistakes. It would be clean-cut.

CHAPTER 5

On the Tiger's Back

My eight days alone, with my pyjamas and dressing-gown, my twenty English cigarettes and my fat volumes of much looked at but little read Dickens and Tolstoy, softened me up considerably, as they were no doubt intended to. I would have welcomed a Leopard Man.

When a visitor did come he was a white-haired, dignified and polite individual—he was introduced as 'the Colonel' and I was to meet him on several occasions in the future. He had with him an interpreter—Alex—and they quickly got down to the business of taking me to pieces, with the eventual aim of sticking me together again so that I looked more like the structure they had in mind for the future career they intended me to follow.

The Colonel began by reading out to me, from a note-book, my own biography up to date. He seemed to know a great deal about me, but the part before I was enrolled as a member of the Communist Party in England was vague and inaccurate. It was rather a shock to me to find that my Communist friends in England had been so painstaking in keeping note of activities which I did not think were any of their business. The thing that interested the Colonel most, after the trivialities had been disposed of, was the differences of opinion I had with Communists in Leicester about Communist tactics and propaganda in and about Africa. It was these differences that had led to my parting company with the Communists temporarily in 1950. I was able and eager to tell the Colonel all about this. I had such a deep conviction that the Communists were right that I felt that all I had to do was to tell them the facts as I saw them about Africa for them to adapt their methods.

These conversations with the Colonel and Alex no doubt served the Russians well enough in making up their minds about what they were going to do with me. But my own need to assert myself had become stronger and I began to protest, vigorously and continuously, and to make all sorts of requests.

This made about as much impression on the Russians as machine-gun fire would make on the armour plating of a battleship, or a water pistol on a whale. The Russians were much more skilful at playing the game of question and answer than I was. They said I must have patience. My requests had to be transmitted to Moscow, and, of course, Moscow had a good many things to do and could not be pressed unduly.

Another character, Major Serge, now made more frequent appearances and it was now either with him or the Colonel that I began to engage in general discussions. We talked about world affairs. We talked about economics, and the Marxist interpretations. I had a good deal to say about the economic situation in Nigeria, with special regard, of course, to the effects of the colonial régime. My Russian friends showed a great deal of interest and both of them thought it would be a good thing if I wrote a report on the economic situation in Nigeria. I didn't mind talking about the economic situation in Nigeria, but writing a report is a different matter since it was quite obvious, despite the flattering implications of the request that it was intended to take my mind off my demands and protests. But after as much shuffling and wasting of time as I could contrive, in the end I had to write the report. It was received with warm thanks and an assurance that it would be put to good use. Maybe it was, but I never heard, one way or the other.

One of the requests I had been making was to be released and allowed to go home. It was at this point that my captors began to atke the line that it was quite impossible for me to go home because the Western press had published stories about my disappearance to the Communist part of Europe. My character was totally blackened. If I returned to England or Nigeria, I would be punished with the brutality characteristic of capitalist societies. The obvious asylum for a man with a blackened character, blackened in this to them virtuous way, was the Soviet Union. I was then specifically invited to write a letter asking permission to go to the USSR.

I was by that time becoming fairly truculent. I said it was too cold in the Soviet Union, I wouldn't do it. My refusal, which I stuck to, annoyed my captors very much indeed and it was followed by two months of dreary solitude, a repetition of my first eight days, only infinitely more painful. But, even so, the old hot and cold technique was applied, because I still had access to all the classics of the nations—and to the standard works of Marxism, Leninism and Stalinism with which the villa was plentifully equipped.

Then they tried me again with another tactic. My interrogators came with a large map of the world and pointed out to me the portion which stretched all the way from the South China seas to the Western border of the East German Republic. Their thesis was the general one that it was inevitable that all other countries, in the end, some soon and some late (but not very late) would fall into the same category. Against this general and, to me at that time, not undesirable background, they pointed specially to Africa and South America which were destined to fall into the Communist orbit almost immediately. With careful detail they enlarged upon the classic situation in these two territories which made their prophecy infallible. Marxism and Leninism was, after all, a science which made it possible to predict these things, unlike the blundering processes of capitalism and imperialism.

They had, therefore, mapped out a future for me. The best thing for me, they said, as an African with the wisdom and experience to accept their point of view, was to use the facilities to which my move to Eastern Germany had opened up for me to equip myself for the time when I would be able to go back to my own country as a potential member of the government in a Socialist (*i.e.* Communist) Nigeria. I would be given all sorts of facilities for academic and technical education, which would accompany the process of equipping me to take part in the evolution of Nigeria as a competent political activist.

They must have felt that at this point they were getting somewhere for the stick was changed for the carrot. The carrot, in this case, was a blonde, pretty and aged, according to her, twenty-four. She began to visit me twice a day for a friendly chat over a cup of coffee and a cigarette—my cigarette, for she did not smoke. She told me she was a Russian and had been born in Gorki and was a graduate of one of Moscow's teacher training colleges. In Germany she was with the Soviet Armed Forces as an education officer.

From the nature of our conversation and the little 'leads' she used to give to it, it did not take me long to realize that she was no more an education officer than I was. I had, as I was to discover more and more frequently in the future, a number of illusions about the Soviet Union, but I had at least heard of the MVD, the Soviet Security Service. My little blonde friend was one of its humbler adjutants.

I welcomed her visits—who wouldn't! But the weeks were passing and I felt that my situation was getting worse. There was no way out by protesting and complaining and demanding things that no one was going to give me. I came to the conclusion, slowly and reluctantly, that I would have to break the deadlock by pretending to accept the terms I had been offered. I realized with my inner mind that pretending to accept them was, for all practical purposes, much the same as simply accepting them. I hinted as much and up came at once the old request that I should write a letter addressed to the Soviet Foreign Ministry asking for permission to visit the Soviet Union. I wrote the letter this time.

But I did not then go to the Soviet Union. What I did not realize then was that this letter of mine was a document essential to my captors who were, at this point, contemplating letting me loose, comparatively speaking, by putting me into the hands of the East German Communists about whose competence and basic loyalty to the Soviet Union they had reservations. My letter to the Soviet Foreign Ministry was, in effect, a request for political asylum. If any difficulties arose in the future, while I was in East German hands, the Russians could claim on the evidence of this document that it was I who had asked for asylum, not they who had kidnapped me. And it was not the last time I had to write such a letter for the record.

Three weeks after my letter—in the spring of 1953—I was in Bautzen with Moroccans, Algerians, Somalis, Syrians, Englishmen, Frenchmen and Americans. I had a new fictitious life history, a new name—I was no longer Ajao; I was Adelani—a new identity. I was one of the considerable band of people like myself, mostly from Afro-Asian countries, who were to be trained as propagandists and activists to further Communist subversion in their own countries.

CHAPTER 6

Double Values

In the end I came to look on many of my companions of Bautzen as tragic figures. When I first encountered them I was still riding on the horns of my unsolved dilemma and finding the process rather exciting. I was annoyed and ruffled by the confinement I had suffered, easy though it was physically, and I resented the frustration of my wishes. After all, the general impression the Russians tried to give, while at the same time keeping their thumbs very firmly on me, was that I was a valuable asset whose benefit was also theirs. They tried to give me the impression that the only differences between us were minor ones concerned with method and timing.

Anyway, it was with a sense of released eagerness that I found myself with a group of young men of many races, who were gathered in Bautzen. Their existence at that moment was a comfort to me and did a great deal to remove my sense of isolation. I was evidently not a freak or a madman since all these other people sympathized with Communism, were trying to understand its ultimate purposes and were eager to see their own countries put on the right road.

It was only slowly that I learned that in a good many of these people (including myself, in the end) the Communists had not made a very good bargain. Among the chosen, or self-chosen, were a much larger proportion of neurotics, misfits, dimwits and so forth than are to be found in any average cross-section of humanity. There were among them, all the same, a fair number of very clever characters ready and able to play their part in Communist 'front' organizations, claiming to represent their own countries, or as activists in party cells on their return to their own countries. But these reflections came later.

My translation to Bautzen, when it came, came suddenly. The

44

Colonel told me that I was to be handed over to the German authorities *immediately*, in the next hour. They would not tell me how long I was to be in Bautzen and what would happen when I got there. My clothes and bag were given back to me. I was given 450 East German marks, worth about £50. The Colonel in his little parting speech said that he required of me that I should keep absolutely secret everything that had happened to me while at Potsdam—making it seem that he was appealing to my sound sense as well as to my proper fear of what might happen if I failed to obey. The Russian Communists, evidently, didn't place too much trust in the German Communists.

I spoke about my mixed feelings. Among them was the hope that the greater freedom (as I saw it) at Bautzen might enable me to let my complaint about my confinement be broadcast to the world. I might even be able to escape. With a part of me I wanted to get back to the freedom even of the capitalist West: and with another I was curious to find out what would happen if I stayed. To Bautzen, then, I went. In a closely curtained car, which I now had a precedent for accepting as one of the customs of the country.

Bautzen is in Saxony and lies on the River Spree. I have a mild passion for guide-books and found out something of Bautzen's ancient and remarkable history. The Wends, a Slav tribe, founded the town in the twelfth century and although swamped by Germanic peoples in the succeeding centuries, it is the place where the Wendish national minority group still lives.

One of the facts I noted was that in the nineteenth century, Bismarck chose Bautzen as the place to build an enormous prison for political offenders. This prison was considerably enlarged by Hitler, in the way dictators have of thinking one cannot have too much of a good thing, and the Russians have added to it still further so that now it is the size of a small town.

Apart from the value of Bautzen as a prison, the Russians also had an interest in the Wendish minority as instruments of propaganda since the Wends had over the years resisted every effort to Germanize them and had, in consequence, suffered much under the Hitler régime. Before the war the Russians found among the Wends useful anti-German sentiments and, cashing in on old associations after the war, they promised the Wends that they would be allowed to set up an autonomous Wendish State if they co-operated in undermining the Germans and breaking up their social structure. The unhappy Wends were also used to help the Russians when they were dismantling East German heavy industries and taking the machinery in train loads back to the Soviet Union to be reconstructed there. The Wends were convinced that in doing so they were helping to fight Fascism.

I am anticipating in my narrative at this point, but the Wends eventually had to learn the hard way that the promises the Communists made to them were valueless. The autonomous State failed to materialize. The Wendish leader, Dr Zieschank, took the hazardous step in 1954 of reminding the Russians of their promise. All he gained was his dismissal from his post as Chairman of the County Council. This was his reward for his work for Communism since his youth, for his political activity in his university, for his nine years in a Nazi concentration camp and for his nine years' co-operation with the Russians after the Second World War. Poor Zieschank had contracted a terrible disease, national chauvinism, and had to be taken out of circulation lest he should infect others with his complaint.

But all that is by the way: and indeed my attitude to the Russians at that time, despite the annoyance I felt at having been coerced by them, was not such that I could believe them guilty of crudities of this kind. The whole body of impressions I had been given of the Russians excluded any other notion than that it was other people, imperialists, colonialists and capitalists, never Communists, who were indifferent to the preservation of human rights. I was a perfect example of someone who believed what he had been told more than three times.

In Bautzen my life began to take on the general pattern it was to keep for some considerable time thereafter. I was given technical instruction of various kinds, mainly concerned with mechanical engineering, with a certain amount of physics, chemistry and mathematics thrown in. And there were, of course, German lessons.

On the practical side I was employed in the Bautzen locomotive factory, where I worked on one of the shifts making wagons. I was told, although not by any of the party functionaries, that the factory before the war produced three hundred wagons a month. In the 1950s it was producing thirty-two wagons a month. The Russians had taken away all the machinery and the workers were left with not much more than hand tools. I worked in the factory two days a week for eight months. Incidentally, I came back to the factory in 1954 for a second spell in different circumstances, but I shall deal with that later (Chapter 13).

The reader may well feel that there is something mysterious and inexplicable about all this. If the Communists wanted to train me as a subversive political agent in Nigeria or as someone they could present as a Nigerian at international propaganda meetings and the like, why did they not get on with it? Why bother to put me in a locomotive factory? Why bother to send me to a technical training school and, having sent me there, never let me finish anything but keep promising me a university training and then withdrawing their promise or, at any rate, not fulfilling it?

When all these things were happening to me I never really analysed the Communists' motives. Looking back now, I can more easily see how much sheer incompetence affected the course of events, and how much—and this applies to all people from abroad in the same category as myself—was due to the uneasy relations between the Soviet and the German Communists.

I still cannot work it out completely. No doubt the ultimate end of the Communist scheme for us was to exploit us in the furtherance of Communist interests in our own countries or in international 'front' organizations like the International Union of Students. But first of all they had to build up some sort of cover story to account for our being there at all.

The letter I wrote after so much argument asking to go to Moscow was no doubt intended to give me the status of a political refugee from imperialism and colonialism. I, an African, oppressed by the imperialists had sought refuge in a Communist country where there was no exploitation, no colour discrimination and no colonialism. (At that time I had never even heard of what happened to the minorities, and the nationalist movements in Soviet Central Asia.)

Another important aspect of my cover-story was that I, as a 'colonial' African, having sought in vain, despite the expenditure of large sums of money, the means of completing my education would be given a free education at the highest university standard by the benevolent Communists.

Looking at it from the Communists' point of view, although I could not be expected to see it in that light, it would take the Communists some time to make up their minds about whether I would 'do' or not. The process of indoctrination and training would necessarily be a long one and since I had not been exactly docile, it might take longer than usual in my case. If I was a doubtful asset because of my argumentative disposition, my history of disagreement with the British Communist Party about Africa and my attitude that I had been spirited into the territory unwillingly and by false pretences, all added up to the notion—not mine but theirs—that the carrot of further education should be continuously dangled before me in order to provide adequate time for sizing me up.

The uneasy relationship between the Russians and the Germans must also have led to a good deal of fumbling and uncertainty, to changes of policy about our use. The result of all this was that during all my time in their hands I was faced with evasiveness and plain lying. The effect of this on my own attitude is difficult for me to assess from the inside, but certainly I came to be the sort of person who always in the first instance suspected the honesty and intentions of everybody. The whole atmosphere in which I lived was one of suspicion and distrust.

The Communists, for one thing, distrusted one another, especially among the rank-and-file. And many of them were not, of course, real Communists at all but were merely men doing their best to survive in adverse circumstances. Higher up, membership of the party, if properly handled, could lead to positions of power and there the wolfish attitude was at its strongest, although less overt.

My companions were a strange mixture of people, as I have said. I formed friendships among them inevitably, some of them warm friendships. Illusory or not, in some of us there was a bond of idealism that helped to keep us in sympathy.

I know very well that people who will lend themselves to exploitation by the Communists in this way are readily dismissed by opponents of Communism as fools, half-baked adolescents or mentally perverted criminals; but this is much too crude. The Communists' methods may be crude but they are not so crude as that. They appeal to the uncertainties as well as to the certainties of youth. A young man has a natural instinct to go contrary to his parents and by extension to the government under which he lives. An external authority which encourages him to believe that his opposition is right and proper and backs up its encouragement with an all-embracing 'scientific' political theory, is in a fair way to obtaining his allegiance. A young man quite often feels a desire to take part in the reformation of the world, and if he is told very firmly that there is only one way, the Communist way, to do it, he will be impressed, especially since the Western democracies' comparable message is vague, unexciting and conservative, rather than dynamic. The Communists have many advantages in these matters and the West should be thankful that they are sometimes not more skilful than they are in taking advantage of them.

In the factory where, among other things, I was supposed to observe the solidarity of the workers under Communism, I had opportunities to meet Germans and to discover just how much they accepted the Communist thesis at its face value. As my German improved, my acquaintance widened. Contacts were slow and uneasy. The Germans knew that an African working in the factory must have been brought there by the party apparatus (and by the Russian, not the German, bit of it) and they were not going to rush up to me with immediate offers to tell me all that was in their minds. So it was a slow business.

But I had plenty of time. I began to find out what the average East German worker really felt about his liberation from capitalist oppression.

CHAPTER 7

The Curtain and the Truth

Gunther M. was about twenty-five. He was a fitter in a Bautzen factory, highly skilled, and a member of a family with a long history of active trade unionism. I knew Gunther and his family for about six months before it became possible for us to exchange a real opinion, or as near to that as either of us ever felt able to go. This was a period of six months in which I was busily, though largely unconsciously, modifying my own opinion. At this time my inclination was to believe that German workers could only benefit from a Communist régime. Gunther's opinion, I gradually discovered, was shared by similar young men I encountered later throughout Eastern Germany; and I even heard the same thing later, although expressed more guardedly, in Moscow.

After we had known each other for quite a long time, Gunther said to me one day, 'Ade, you live in a British colony. Are you really certain that you Nigerians are worse off than we Germans are?'

The very fact that he could ask himself, let alone me, such a question, struck me as remarkable. But Gunther and I had got to the stage when a friendship had developed which we both seemed to feel was based on affection as well as mutual respect and trust, although I doubt if one can ever speak about complete trust in a country controlled by a multitude of secret intelligence and counter-intelligence groups always spying on one another.

I had now been in the Communist world for nearly eighteen months. I had more than once visited Gunther's family. I knew that his grandfather had taken an active, perhaps a leading part in the trade union movement in Germany. His father was an 'Old Communist', meaning a man who had been a member of the Communist Party in the 1920s. He—Gunther's father—had left the Communist Party, or the Socialist Unity Party (SED) as it is now called in East Germany, in 1947. His own version—he would say no more to me—was that he found it impossible to reconcile with his conscience what the party wanted him to do in post-war Germany.

His resignation was a brave action because as a result of it he was thrown out of his factory job and saved from gaol only because the Communists were frustrated by the widespread resentment among his fellow-workers in the factory which at that time they could not afford to ignore.

The Communists did not stop at Gunther's father, but visited his 'sins' on the next generation. Gunther had completed his secondary education after the war and had passed with reasonable credit the entrance examination for the mechanical engineering school at Bautzen. He had been refused admission to the engineering school on the grounds that his father was a branded Titoist, that is, he was a Communist infected with nationalism. Because of this condemnation of his father Gunther considered himself lucky to have a job as a lathe-operator earning an average of about 240 marks a month (about £25). Wage figures are meaningless if they are not related to their purchasing power. In Bautzen at that time a pair of shoes cost £12 10s., half Gunther's monthly wage.

Gunther and his family, because of their quarrel with the Communist Party, were, in a sense, exceptional, and I was even then up to a point prepared to discount their criticisms of the régime. But later I learned that their views were widely shared with those who had no similar experience. And much later, when I was at Leipzig University, I learned that it was commonplace for children to suffer in this way. If the Communist authorities wished to get rid of or punish a student, they could always invent some action by the previous generation if it suited their book to do so.

I hesitated to answer Gunther's question, which shows that although we were real friends, there were forbidden zones. It was very bold of Gunther to ask the question and perhaps knowing some of my uncorrected enthusiasms at that time, he may have expected me to pour out the familiar party-line or to produce a row of statistics showing how enormously better off those living under Communism were compared with the down-trodden victims of imperialism in Africa. I was fairly well equipped with

Communist jargon by this time—the evening seminars in Marxism and Leninism at Bautzen had produced their fruits in season, and I knew well about the orthodox view of statistics as a weapon of propaganda. I knew the quotations from Lenin and those of lesser pundits like Togliatti.

But I was not prepared to use the weapon on Gunther, because I was by no means sure it would 'work' and I knew that he really wanted to know the answer. He wanted to learn about other countries without the screen of the Communist Party between the question and the answer. This desire is widespread among East German and Soviet youths who are very much aware of their isolation behind the Iron Curtain. They want to find out the real conditions of people, especially their contempories, in the world outside the Communist orbit.

They have lost faith (if indeed they ever had it) in their own press and radio. This is particularly true of some of the industrial workers who hear the production figures of their own factory grossly inflated for propaganda purposes. These young men want very much to learn about other parts of the world and to compare what they know with what is kept from them.

So, in the end, I found myself telling Gunther all about my own country, and its relations with Britain. Even then, I was careful not to go too far in contradicting the party-line because I had no wish to get either myself or Gunther into trouble with the Secret Police should our conversation be reported.

Of course, I was convinced that the colonial régime, however gentle the hands of our rulers, was fundamentally wrong and must come to an end and I believed that my country was economically exploited and that essential industrialization would never take place while it remained in the interests of the British to extract our raw materials and at the same time ensure that the Nigerians did not become competitive manufacturers. But in this moment of truth, if that is what it was in spite of its limitations, I told Gunther that even under imperialism the individual enjoyed freedom which appeared to be unkown in Eastern Germany. I pointed out that in Nigeria a visitor would never be restricted, as I was at that particular moment in Germany, to a radius of travel of 25 kilometres from my place of residence. And it would never happen, so far as I knew, that a skilled worker with a family to look after, would have imposed on him a fifty per cent.

cut in his wages because he disagreed with the government on a point of policy.

This conversation seemed to clear the air and put our friendship on an easier basis. I do not blame Gunther and his family for their reticences. It was in this conversation, or soon after, that Gunther's father began to talk more freely about his past experiences. For nearly twenty years his obstinacy, which is another word for sticking to his principles, had kept him in trouble, first with the Hitler régime and afterwards with the Communists. He was a modest man and would say very little about his own actions. With him it was the trade union movement all the time. It was only with difficulty that I could persuade him even to mention his years in the concentration camp.

One would think that a man who had been imprisoned by Hitler had seen the worst. But it was not so, and he had been left, when I knew him, with the firm conviction that, from the workers' point of view, the worst that capitalism and Fascism had been able to do fell far short of what was being experienced by the workers under the East German Communist administration, which he described as a puppet government set up by Moscow and maintained in power by Russian tanks. When I got to know more about what had happened in 1953 during the workers' rising, I had more understanding of what Gunther's father meant when he talked about the role of the Soviet tank in the borderlands of the Soviet orbit.

I am very much aware, in writing about industrial relations in Eastern Germany, that although I had an unusual opportunity to see what went on, my range of vision was necessarily narrow. Specialists who have had an opportunity to study what went on in detail have succeeded in dealing with the matter much more completely. From my restricted position, therefore, I can do no more than give a personal impression.

My work in the locomotive factory two days a week did not contribute much to the rolling-stock of Eastern Germany. As time went on my participation became even less for I and some other supernumeraries were put on what was called 'waiting time' for two and a half months. This meant that we had to report at the factory at the normal working time and then were taken off in columns, irrespective of grades or qualifications, to do manual work either on a construction site or on the land. We disliked

53

this process in spite of the allurements of fresh air and exercise as a benefit to our bodies and the exalted feeling that we were contributing to the construction of a new society which it was supposed to induce in us. But we resented it even more because it meant a fifty per cent. reduction in our wages. For this the official explanation was that since we were not doing the work of our proper trade, we could not expect to receive our full pay. The trade unions would, quite rightly, object to this. Considering the status of the trade unions as instruments of the government's schemes to increase production, it can be imagined that this argument fell on rather deaf ears.

The government-controlled trade unions and their function in the Communist world are familiar enough, but this was to us a striking instance of showing whose side they were on. The authorities knew that the trade unions were not popular with the workers in Eastern Germany so they provided us with an alternative or additional explanation which was that this waiting time had been caused by 'enemies of the people'.

These 'enemies of the people' were always found when difficulties arose. The purpose of the device was to divert attention from the real causes of any particular trouble in industry and to direct it towards some director or manager, preferably one of non-proletarian origin on whose head the righteous anger of the workers would fall so that the party's or the government's own inefficiency would be concealed. There were troubles enough in all conscience, caused by sheer inefficiency and by the highly disreputable facts of attempts to maintain party discipline.

And, apart from all this, there was a very serious factor which loomed over everything else. This was the large scale—and of course forbidden—emigration of East Germans, especially among just those young men potentially most valuable to the régime, to Western Germany. This emigration was brought about by dissatisfactions that no propaganda could successfully conceal— unsatisfactory conditions in their own country and lack of opportunity.

We saw the cumulative effect of this dissatisfaction one day in June 1953.

CHAPTER 8

The Workers' Revolt

Foreign students in Eastern Germany were expected to focus their minds entirely on their studies, and even during what passed for recreation the notion was never absent that everything they did in some way contributed to fitting them to work for the great cause. All our permitted reading was of material which was either Communist, or sympathetic to it, or happened to foreshadow the triumph of Marxism.

Our lack of access to printed matter which disagreed with the Communist point of view was not so much that we were continuously being warned against or were even forbidden to read it. It simply wasn't there to be read. But somehow all the foreign students seemed to know at once when something unusual was going on inside or outside the Communist area. Perhaps it was only something like the schoolboy's pleasure when his teacher slips on a banana skin, but even among those of us who really did support Communism the discomfiture of the Communist Powers gave us a greater, or at any rate a more rarified, pleasure, than the difficulties of the imperialists.

I, as an African, was very familiar from childhood with the extraordinary ability of primitive peoples to communicate knowledge of events over great distances without the aid of modern devices. In Eastern Germany, I do not suggest there was anything supernatural, as some say there is among Africans, in our ability to find out quickly what was going on. The half-hearted Communism of so many East Germans helped greatly, since, not being imbued with the sense of security which is characteristic of the *apparatchik*, they gossiped all the time. There was a network of gossiping, not in any sense organized, but curiously effective. It was a product of a painful mixture of hope and fear. Many Germans, as the events of 1953 proved, hoped that disaster would befall their leaders. They also feared that something nasty would happen to themselves in the process. The word-of-mouth news that was circulating was often inaccurate on matters of fact but it was rare that it was altogether wrong. When 'something' happened we always knew, even if we did not know precisely what it was. It was rather like the mysterious awareness which prisoners have of what is happening. Murmurs were intelligible, silences often had meanings of their own. The atmosphere seemed to generate, as it does in a cell, a means of communication that can be picked up by the sixth sense developed under pressure. This kind of knowledge was, of course, added to in an unmysterious way—this is true of prison life also—by practical and deliberate systems of conveying information which defy all the authorities can do to stop them.

When I arrived in Bautzen in the early spring of 1953 as a new recruit of a fairly rare type, I was accommodated in the Hotel Holstadt. I had a room of my own which I soon saw was a rare privilege. After a month or so I was moved to lodgings with a German family in Karl Marx Strasse.

At this time my knowledge of German was very limited although I seemed to be learning fairly fast. Many of the foreign students were in the same condition, and we tended to associate with those with whom we shared a common language. I found myself with those who could speak English—though it was not necessarily their mother tongue.

It was an indication of the inefficiency of the supervision that we were not prevented from forming small social groups of this kind on the basis of our sense of isolation from the rest of the community. A good deal of our time was spent grumbling. We discussed the decisions that were made affecting us and we criticized individuals, without inhibition. These student intimacies ranged us on one side, with our instructors and the various people we in due course dealt with in the management of FDJ—the Free German Youth movement—or the trade unions, on the other side. It was a blunder on the part of the authorities, and it must have been due to the early stage of the school's development.

In spite of the unsatisfactory experience of training Africans which my own career helped to illustrate, the Communists must have continued to believe that these schools were worth having because they have been extended and enlarged. I have learned since my return to Nigeria that there are schools with a similar purpose in Budapest, Prague, at Bernau near Berlin and in Warsaw, in addition to the one at Bautzen.

Our course at the International Solidarity School at Bautzen was formally opened on Labour Day, 1953. The opening had been postponed to coincide with May 1st. The students celebrated the opening with a drunken frolic in the evening which got some of them into trouble with the police. We were a very cynical lot and the notion that young Communists behaved like young angels had no appeal for us.

I made friends with a Saarlander, François Schmidt, who had been a member of the French Foreign Legion, and had been taken prisoner by the Communists while fighting for the French in Vietnam. He had come to East Germany through Communist channels, via China. I noticed that his hands had been injured and that he did not have full use of them. I attributed this to injuries inflicted on him while he was a prisoner, but François would never say one way or the other.

One morning in June, François and I were playing table-tennis in the school recreation room where students idled, talked or played games between classes. Suddenly three students burst into the room, obviously excited, and shouted, 'The revolution has broken out. The workers are striking in Berlin and all over East Germany. The radio says Goerlitz is in the hands of escaped political prisoners.'

François and I paid no attention and went on with our game. Nobody else seemed to take any notice. The fact that the students as a whole reacted with indifference, was, in a way, just as remarkable as the arrival of the students with the first news of the East German uprisings. François and I knew the three students and put down their announcement to student leg-pulling. Instinctively, perhaps, we were being careful not to associate ourselves with any particular attitude to these events.

We thought no more about the matter during classes but in the early evening François and I set off together. We lodged in different parts of Bautzen and had formed the habit of escorting each other to our respective digs on alternate days. My lodgings in Karl Marx Strasse were reached by way of the Red Army Square. When we got there we could see at once that something unusual was going on. In those days the inhabitants of Bautzen went to and fro about their affairs quietly and unobtrusively. They did not gather in groups about the streets, even on summer evenings.

But on this evening there were groups of men here and there about the square talking, with their heads together, moving from group to group and obviously intensely excited about something. By this time François and I realized that what we had heard earlier in the day really meant something. François, whose German was better than mine, asked one group what it was all about. They seemed to resent his questions, told him to mind his own business and muttered something about trouble in Berlin.

François and I made our separate ways to our digs. I had a wireless set and I tuned in, as I often did, to AFN. The American station reported that in many places throughout Eastern Germany disturbances had broken out. The strike of the workers on a building site in the Stalinallee in East Berlin over increased norms and cuts in pay, had sparked off similar action in over three hundred towns and villages. It looked as if the students' story of the morning might well lead to a breakdown of government and the end of the Communist régime in East Germany. My room faced the street and by hanging out of the window I could see what was going on in Red Army Square. I jumped about between my wireless set and my window. In the square I could see that larger crowds were gathering.

Eventually I went out and walked to the square. It was the same as it had been earlier in the day except that there were far more people, all talking and gesticulating in little groups. There was no organized demonstration and no public speaking. While I moved about in the crowd, groups of uniformed police on foot came into the square and, without using force, urged the people to disperse. This had no effect, and it was obvious that stronger action by the authorities would follow since the crowd was getting to a point when a leader would emerge and organize it. I had no wish to get mixed up in any local troubles. What had they to do with me, after all? So I slid back to my lodgings and took up my position again at the window.

The crowd was coming to the boil. The failure of the police to disperse the crowd produced its sequel. First one armoured car manned by Russians appeared, then three or four more. They drove into Red Army Square quite fast and began to move in circles. The crowd at first did not seem to take them too seriously. They ran on to pavements and up side streets and then came back into the square.

This situation lasted no more than a few minutes. The armoured cars converged on the centre of the square, faced outwards, re-angled their machine guns and fired several rounds into the air. That was enough. The crowd went, and the square was empty.

The next morning was one of the days when certain students, including myself, went for our practical training at the Bautzen locomotive factory. But there was something new at the factory. It was guarded by soldiers armed with sub-machine guns. Inside the factory there was no strike so far as I was ever able to discover, and there were no demonstrations, but the workers were restive and expectant.

During the period which followed, restrictions were everywhere imposed. In the school announcements were made forbidding public assembly and imposing a curfew. It was a period of great nervous strain for the whole community. We knew, as we realized later, all the essential details about the German uprising. The local SED and SSD (State Security Police) men knew them too and it had a certain sinister fascination for us to watch their reaction. Some of them quietly put away the party symbols which they wore or carried, and in their conversation there were many evasions.

One of the most interesting phenomena of this period was the readjustment of the party-line. All these events are now receding so much into the past that it is difficult to recall them. But I remember clearly enough that it was not long before this that the East German authorities had taken the unusual step of admitting publicly that many of their policies had been incorrect and unsuccessful. The whole atmosphere in East Germany was filled with recriminations and admissions of errors. The formal action on the part of the authorities was to lay down a 'New Course' which was intended to cure the faults. In our situation as students, we knew a good deal about what had happened to members of certain youth organizations, such as those connected with the Protestant churches, who had been thrown out of secondary schools. We knew that students had been expelled from universities because they had the wrong attitude or the wrong social origins. The authorities had promised to review these decisions.

At a deeper level, we knew that the main sources of the régime's difficulties were economic, and that the industrial workers as a whole had the acutest reasons for dissatisfaction. When the demonstrations and strikes blew up in the middle of June, their primary purpose was to demand better working conditions, especially better pay and the reduction of the normal output required.

But this bubbling up of the workers' resentment quickly produced the wider demand that the whole régime should be modified, that the government should resign and that a new one should take its place as a result of free elections. Resentment was also directed especially against the People's Police, the disguised army maintained in barracks and evidently designed for the twin purpose of quelling popular resentment if it took an active form and of establishing the basis of a new army.

What happened in Goerlitz, from which news of one of the earliest outbreaks had fallen on our deaf ears, was typical. There demonstrations had begun at the Lowa Works early in the morning of June 17th. The demonstrators had marched through the town and had stopped at the Rathaus to seize the Communist burgomaster and force him to march in the demonstration. The demonstrators formed themselves into groups to seize the headquarters of Communist-controlled organizations like the House of German-Soviet Friendship. The SED headquarters was entered and a party secretary beaten up. At the SSD building the crowd demanded the release of political prisoners. SSD men were set upon and beaten up.

In the afternoon of the same day a crowd of many thousands assembled in Goerlitz and formed an action committee. This committee decided to submit demands to East Berlin for free elections, for the resignation of the government, for the dissolution of the People's Police and for the release of food supplies from police stores. The committee then advised the strikers to return to work. At 4 p.m. Russian armoured cars appeared, seized the town hall, dispersed the crowds and took over. Martial Law was declared.

All over East Germany the order of events was similar.

Our school of instruction continued throughout this period. Our first session every morning in the International Solidarity School was a study of the day's news as reported in Communist news-

60

papers. Our discussion was supervised by Herr Martinglocke who was the school's social science (i.e. Marxist-Leninist) instructor.

In the few days immediately after the June disturbances the party-line was by no means clear and Herr Martinglocke made a very poor attempt to give the clear dogmatic and unarguable views to which we were accustomed. We students were still untutored in the niceties of the Communist conception of 'free' discussion, and we fired off a number of direct and extremely sceptical questions at our instructor.

In the absence of the correct party-line Herr Martinglocke took as his starting point the 'New Course' announced by the East German Politburo earlier in June and was quite prepared to concede that the German workers had genuine grievances which it was the duty of the government to meet. The workers, although misguided in their methods, were quite right to demand that food supplies should be improved and that more consumer goods should be obtainable. This gave us excellent openings for argument and we used them to the full. But in a few days the line hardened and there was no more talk about justifiable grievances. The demonstrations were 'the work of Fascist agents infiltrated from the West' who worked with 'bourgeois remnants' inside the Democratic Republic. There were no permissible arguments against that, even by skilful users of the dialectic.

In Bautzen, as elsewhere in East Germany, ultimate authority and power was in the hands of the Russians, not the Germans. Foreign students who got into trouble during this period, even for the mildest offences, were not dealt with by the German police, but by the Russian Stadt Kommandatura.

CHAPTER 9

I Try to Escape

East German propaganda made great efforts to show that those who went to the West were useless remnants of a bourgeois or Fascist society to which the West was more than welcome. But in hard fact the large-scale movement caused an acute shortage of labour in a great many sectors of the East German economy.

In agriculture and construction the situation was particularly bad. A year after my first attempted escape the government introduced legislation which made it compulsory for all those leaving school to do up to one years' manual labour or to serve in the armed forces before they would be considered for enrolment in a university. This legislation was merely the very belated formalization of a practice in operation in other forms for years.

I do not see what one can call this system except forced labour, however much it is wrapped up in propaganda. The Communists not only wrapped up their own practices of this sort in propaganda, but they busied themselves in condemning forced labour, as they made out it was practised by everyone except the Communists.

School-leavers were, in effect, conscripted, for there was no escape from it. It was universally detested, although of course the party was always able to produce the necessary young zealot who was prepared to say that his labour was enobling and was willingly contributed to bring about a better, more Communist world. The students detested it for its own sake, but they also deeply resented the fact that it interrupted their studies and had no relevance to them. The practice did not stop there because, even after they were enrolled in universities or technical colleges, they were repeatedly asked to fill labour gaps.

The Communists, indeed, went farther than Hitler's Minister of Labour, Dr Ley, because they made use of what was, for all practical purposes, child labour under the guise of practical work in the course of a polytechnic education. Dr Ley is, no doubt, turning in his grave with regret that he did not think of this, and Marx and Engels are no doubt doing the same thing, for different reasons, considering their strictures on the use of child labour in British industry in the nineteenth century.

My worries were by no means confined to social or political philosophy. I was fed up, disgruntled, couldn't stand it any more. My main aim, now that I was in the net, of getting myself useful education, was being frustrated. I do not know when the idea of trying to get out of the Communist area first began to take form in my mind, but by the beginning of 1954 it was clear enough. And I was not alone—unfortunately as it turned out—in my wish to get away.

Looking back on it, our attempt was foredoomed to failure. There were four of us, all harbouring God knows what inner suspicions of each other's honesty, who began to find out that there was enough common ground between us to plan an escape from East Germany. There was Pierre the Frenchman, van der Post the Dutchman, Mossman the American Jew and myself. Too many, obviously, and we were not very experienced. We started at the beginning, instead of using the experience of others to guide and warn us. It was typical of the whole atmosphere in which we lived that we should have gone about the matter so amateurishly.

It is necessary to think of the foreign students being trained in Communism, in combination with sporadic education, not only as a composite group, but as a group that had little groups within it. The Communists were generally rather clever about dealing with the little groups. They had names for them all: the Left and Right deviationists, the nationalists, the revisionists and so forth, and usually when they detected a tendency to stray from the path of orthodoxy they tried persuasion to bring the wanderers back.

But at the back of the persuasion there were stronger forces, and plenty of them. We were left in no doubt about that, and there was a sense of oppression in all our activities. The whole atmosphere was, in fact, poisoned by fear and suspicion. It is a thing difficult to describe, although it is easier to do so in some ways after it is all over than it would have been at the time.

We were all, in some way and in different degrees, attached to the notion that Communism had the secret of power and of ultimate victory over other political forces. This notion made us able, up to a point, to accept a considerable lessening of our individual liberty, mental and physical. There was a sense that Communists, the German ones, had quite enough power to deal with the local situation, and that even if they were occasionally feeble, or incompetent, there was still, beyond them, the immensely powerful, ruthless and somewhat mysterious Russians, who as far as we were concerned were sparing of their presence, but very impressive and sometimes frightening when they did appear.

Pierre, 'van', Mossman and I somehow found ourselves beginning to share our miseries. We began by simple grumbling, and found that we grumbled in the same way, and about the same things. We did not like our conditions, although I at any rate had little to grumble about on that score, since I was billeted in a respectable (this is not a phrase the Communists would approve of) petty bourgeois household where I was comfortable, and I had 300 marks a month, which was enough for my needs, if it gave me little margin.

Our dissatisfaction, as the habit of talking together grew, began to take a more serious form. We began, not only to grumble about our frustrated educational training, but about the very foundations of our being with the Communists at all. Doubts about the dogma, in other words, and we became guilty of serious heresies. There were many groups like our own. It was, now I look back on it, an indication that the Communists still had a good deal to learn about how to detach potentially useful people from non-Communist countries permanently. We four were no more remarkable than any of the others. We had for various reasons found ourselves swept into the machine, and our temperaments, and individual desires had not been successfully ironed out.

As we talked, and as we commiserated with each other about our troubles, we managed to convince ourselves that there was no future for us, and that the best thing to do was to clear out. But how? Obviously it was no good asking the authorities to let us go, although it might have been possible to argue, in any non-Communist situation, that they were in fact not going to find us worth our keep. Nor was it a question of going off in a train to Berlin, despite the fact that there were trains and there was, apparently, nothing to stop us buying tickets. Nor was it likely to be easy for me, as an African, to expect to get to the frontier with Western Germany, where the flow of refugees was large, without being noticed by

someone who would make it his business to point me out to the
authorities. A taxi? Some people, I had heard, had managed to
get to the frontier by hiring a taxi. This would cost money, but it
might be possible to save up enough to pay for it. At that time
there were still a few private enterprise vehicles for hire, although
most had been taken over by the State. And, of course, it was more
than likely that the 'free' taxi-men included a sprinkling of *agents
provocateurs*. How was one to know? Whom could one trust?
Yes, we were evidently amateurs. Anyway, could we trust our
quartet not to include a spy?

We began to go into details. Train to Berlin seemed the best
answer. But by what route? The alternatives were to try to go to
Berlin by slow train direct from Bautzen, or to go somewhere else
first, and try to get to Berlin from there. We came to the conclusion
that the best thing to do would be to go to Leipzig first, and go
from there to our goal. We would be unknown there, there was a
bigger population and our movements would be less noticeable.
And, of course, we did not propose to set off looking like people
going on a long journey.

We had it all worked out. For weeks we accumulated money.
We sold unobtrusively (or so we thought) cameras or wireless sets,
if we happened to have them: and we planned to leave Bautzen
taking only the kind of food which could be explained away as
intended for a picnic. We were hard-up students, who couldn't
afford to eat in hotels and restaurants but we thought it quite
possible that we might have to go into hiding and would need a
supply of food to keep us going.

All this took time, and there was endless talk, endless argument,
and when we had decided on the day we would make our attempt
we were still uncertain about what we would do when we got to
Leipzig. And we might never get there, of course. I had found out,
quite by accident, that there were road-blocks all round Bautzen,
and there might well be train checks.

The road-blocks came to my knowledge one night when I had
been out of Bautzen with a group of FDJ members engaged in 'agitation in the countryside', which was part of our training. Somehow
in walking away from the village to catch the last train to Bautzen
our bear-leader took the wrong turning, and we suddenly found
ourselves, a mixed group of foreigners led by a bad-tempered
German who had lost his way, face to face with a road barricade

manned by very suspicious and rough-tongued soldiers armed with stubby light machine-guns, steadily directed at our bellies. We explained ourselves, sufficiently to avoid anything more serious than being turned back. But we were suspect enough even then for us to need a military escort to see that we did not get lost again. We had missed the last train, and we had to walk fourteen miles, soldiers included. I remember it well.

Our decision to try to escape was a bold enterprise. Our departure from Bautzen would be discovered at once. Our hope was that no one would know where we had gone. Fond hope.

The day came, a busy Saturday when our absence from school did not arise, and when students, even dedicated souls like ourselves, could relax, could even go off on little excursions by train without being automatically suspected of treachery. We tried to look as innocent as our natures and appearance allowed. Our little picnic parcels looked like many others.

We knew exactly what we were going to do. Hans would go to the ticket office, get in the queue and buy four tickets to Leipzig. We would wait nearby chatting as gaily as we could about nothing in particular. It all went off very well. We could see nothing likely to lead to trouble. There were lots of people about, many looking just like ourselves, students on an outing.

Hans reached the grill. We could see him speak, hand over the money and get the tickets. He stepped out of the queue, and came towards us, everything normal and natural.

And then, over his shoulder, I saw two men come up behind him. They took Hans's arms, one on each side, and steered him towards us. Black leather coats, caps, boots. SSD.

It was all too simple. Prods in our ribs with hard objects. Peremptory gestures of the head and gloved fingers. It was all over in a moment. We were out of the station, a closely packed little group, too dismayed to utter more than words of feeble protest based on our role of picnickers, probably, indeed certainly, lacking in conviction, and into a closed van, in no more than a minute. That was my escape.

It had serious, but in some ways rather curious consequences. I never saw any of my companions again. Who betrayed us I never knew, except that I had not done so.

I had a rough time in the hands of the SSD. It was the first time, and in fact the only time, I was actually ill-treated physically during my stay behind the Iron Curtain. It *was* an Iron Curtain for me this time. I was in the cellars below the SSD headquarters, on straw, and not much of it, on a dirty stone floor. It was cold and damp.

I was interrogated, endlessly. But not beaten, not tortured, not brainwashed. And in a couple of weeks, I was released. I stuck to my picnic story, but without very much conviction.

It was pretty rough, but I did not somehow feel that I was in any serious danger of being eliminated. I knew that trying to run away was a grave offence, because it was a nuisance to the authorities, and if I was likely to talk too much after I got away it might be damaging to their propaganda.

My German captors' methods were not particularly skilful or persistent. They were rough and ready, unimaginative, crude, and in a way, indifferent. They were not deeply concerned about me and my fate one way or another. They weren't prepared to take a great deal of trouble either for me or against me.

The Russians were different. They took everything much more seriously, and were prepared to show patience and skill in dealings with the least of their servants. They really were Communists, unlike the Germans, who for the most part were trying to survive by refraining from crossing swords with the new régime. I was not charged with any crime. I was merely kept locked up in considerable discomfort, and fed on disgusting and unsatisfying food.

And then I was let out. It was as simple as that. One day the cell was visited by the Russians, who looked at me, talked to me about my studies, and then went off; and the next day I was back in my comfortable billet, with the German shopkeeper and his wife who had taken me in as a lodger because it had been 'suggested' to them that it would be a good thing, and might keep their shop open just a little longer.

But the escapade had a decisive effect on my career as a student. I wanted to go to Leipzig University, but that was 'out' now—I should have to go through a period of penitence and rehabilitation. I was quietly removed from my office as FDJ secretary, on the grounds of ill-health. I went back to work in the locomotive factory—I hadn't much choice—I was running out of money. It may sound fantastic, but apart from this, the only serious rebuke I got after my attempted escape was having it pointed out to me that I had clearly fallen into bad ideological company and was deviating from the true path. The right thing for me, they thought, was a chance to live among the real toilers, to absorb their atmosphere, and to purge my system of false notions derived from my bourgeois background and contacts with unsuitable companions.

The effect of all this on me was not to restore my faith in the system, but simply to make me, as I thought, more cunning. I decided that it was no good attempting to defy authority. It was better to accept that they were smarter than I and that the only hope I had of getting out was to pretend to go along with them, to be a 'good boy'. No point in banging my head against a wall.

But I was angry and disgruntled permanently and nothing that happened thereafter made me anything else. I was still obsessed with the idea of escape, but I was resolved that there would be no more group conspiracies. No one was to be trusted. If I had to get out, I would have to do it alone.

CHAPTER 10

The Doctrine and its Victims

When I had found myself locked up in the villa in Potsdam (see Chapter 5) and realized that my only course was to go on in the way my captors indicated, the appeal that was made to me was primarily that my personal interests lay in accepting the offer of education in Eastern Germany. This prospect was described very glowingly and when I had shown signs of acquiescence those who were looking after me played upon my isolation with great skill. Because I was left alone so much any visitor was welcome simply because he offered a human contact. I was not browbeaten, or called a fool because I argued with them. Looking back on it, their effort, apart from engaging me in discussions about world political issues, was, progressively during the months of my captivity to make the West and all that I had left behind me, seem unreal. They were clearing my mind, making it empty of the impressions I had carried with me.

This aim was largely achieved, and since I was already disposed to think on Communist lines, continuous contact with skilful and apparently well informed and personally agreeable people had a powerful influence on me.

Thus when I left Potsdam for Bautzen, I was, in practice, a convert to the idea that my future lay with the Communists. But I had reservations, serious ones, because I was always conscious that hidden behind the smooth talk and persuasive argument, there were threats. I was told, for instance, that the Western Press had denounced me (this was not true so far as I could ever discover) and that if I attempted to return I would be in serious trouble.

During my life in Bautzen, all sorts of relationships developed with a great variety of people. With my instructors and supervisors there was an uneasy and watchful and yet curiously intimate form of dealing. With my fellow students there was an odd mixture of real friendship and competitive uneasiness. Then there were contacts with people on the factory floor which in turn was mixed up with the whole complex of relationships with the party, the trade unions and with the various party-controlled elements of local government.

The Russians were there, pervasively, although they tried their best to be unobtrusive. All the time I was attending the course of technical instruction at Bautzen, I was continually in touch with some Russian or other—or rather they were in touch with me. It was they who were continually keeping an eye on me and my development as a potential political agent. As far as they were concerned, my engineering and other studies were secondary. They were a means of keeping me busy and out of mischief and were a sort of re-insurance policy.

The particular Russian officer on whose list of candidates I was, was quite prepared to discuss such large matters as Communism's future plans. I remember one day he began to talk to me about how he saw the problem of influencing, for example, West African countries.

'It is easy for us', he said, 'to send to Africa or to other countries we wish to befriend teams of Russian technical and scientific experts, and no doubt that is what we will do when the time is ripe in each place. But it is not so easy for people of that kind or, indeed, for Russian political specialists—party members and so forth—to persuade the natives of such countries to accept dialectical materialism and the historical necessities which it implies for their own societies. We have found, by experience, that this difficulty can readily be overcome, or at least minimized, if the political propaganda is publicly done by natives of the country itself.'

I remember this episode well. It marked a stage in my development as a potential political agent. Such propositions did not, of course, either surprise or shock me. I was interested in them technically.

Officially and outwardly, the Bautzen school's purpose was to give foreign students a training as technicians in industry or to enable them to fit themselves to take further courses at university level elsewhere. But its real purpose was quite simply to deal with the foreign students' minds by firm indoctrination aimed at removing any reservations they might have about Communism and enable them to master Communist thinking and practices in such a way as to make them useful as political instruments. They were trying to produce people who were either active and zealous fighters for Communism or were sufficiently neutralized to be useful as blind and willing Soviet agents.

If I was capable of looking at the Bautzen Solidarity School dispassionately, I would almost begin to feel sorry for its management. They cannot have got very high marks from their Russian masters.

When I was in the school there were about seventy 'students'. Only eight of those managed to survive. Some of my fellow students come back to my mind very vividly. There were the Americans, Victor G. who was later to be trained in publicity methods at the Karl Marx University at Leipzig: there was James R. an intelligence officer in the United States forces who was a Communist sympathizer until he saw the system in practice: Jean C. the Frenchman with the classical education who was a member of the French Communist Party and was to lecture in French at the Karl Marx University: Simon L. with a B.Sc. in chemistry who managed to find his way back to Paris in 1955: and there was Antonio G., the Mexican, and Peter D. from Birmingham, a born mathematician who was assigned to mechanical engineering at Bautzen. He fell into a political dispute with the authorities, was expelled and heard of no more. There was Piet J., the Hollander, who was distinguished from the rest of us by his complete and unquestioning acceptance of the Soviet view of everything. I suppose we all shared a common desire to learn as much as we could from the technical instruction available in the school.

But we were in a firm grip. The only way we could get access to the means of learning something useful was to undergo for three hours daily compulsory lectures on politics and philosophy, of course, on strictly Marxist lines, as well as five hours a week on what they called 'Social Science', also compulsory in Communist seats of learning. (The school did not seek to draw unnecessary attention to the fact that it was giving intensive instruction in Marxism-Leninism and in the use of the dialectical method, so this part of the curriculum was classified as 'Social Science'.)

In these lectures nothing was left to chance, no remnant of

bourgeois capitalist teaching was left uncorrected. We were led through the Russian interpretation of history from the time of the early Pharaohs to the present post-Hiroshima nuclear age. This included a reading of the Communist Manifesto, and a historical description of the state of the world when it was published. From this we were led to the history of the CPSU, which followed the classic Stalinist version, omitting references to such people as Trotsky except in terms of the strongest disapproval. Interwoven in this history of the world, which purported to be a strictly objective (i.e. Marxist) account of events, was a continuous effort to glorify the Soviet achievement. This had no limits, and included Russian achievements that had chronologically nothing to do with Communism but in some mysterious way seemed to be attributable to it at whatever time they occurred.

On another tack we were led through the Hegel-Marx-Lenin philosophical maze. This part of the course was given an air of objectivity by the presentation of highly selective and, in the end, disparaging accounts of the view of misguided philosophers like Kant.

At the morning session, when we discussed the day's news, events were related to what we had been taught in the 'Social Science' course. This was made more effective in my own case for the group which I attended for newspaper reading had as its instructor Herr Martinglocke, who was also the instructor in Marxism-Leninism.

In the early stages before our individual views had been smoothed out, there were frequent disputes between the half-indoctrinated students and the lecturers. We often contradicted the lecturers on matters of fact. I well remember Herr Martinglocke stating baldly that there were more motor cars in Eastern Germany than there were in Federal Germany since socialism necessarily brought about a more prosperous society than was possible in the decadent West. Some of the students were defectors from the West, and whatever their motives in coming to Eastern Germany, statements of this kind were too much for them. They argued as if they had never heard of the correct party method of expressing differences of opinion.

But gradually disputes of this kind ceased, in class at least, where we soon learned that bad marks were recorded against those who entered into arguments of this type. The bad marks were awarded on the perfectly logical basis that even half-trained students should know better than to argue on a non-Marxist basis. If they did, they deserved to be punished.

These arguments sometimes cost students their degrees. For example, Franz D., who was a friend of mine—he obtained his degree somewhat later in Western Germany—blamed his failure to qualify in Eastern Germany on the fact that he had declined to accept the statement by one of his instructors, Professor Ley (later director of a radio network in Eastern Germany), that the steam engine was invented by the Russians and that Lenin had personally invented the tractor.

In Bautzen, by comparison with what went on later in Dresden and Leipzig, instruction was fairly crude, but it was all-pervasive. Not only were we subjected to it in school but when we did our part-time work in the locomotive factory it was continually stressed in our trade union activities. The same was true in the meetings of the FDJ and in its Sport and Technique Section where we received our elementary military training.

In Dresden and Leipzig the whole structure of indoctrination was more academic. When I went to Dresden first, however, I was allowed to absent myself from the initial classes because my marks had been good in Bautzen.

The political course in Dresden put the emphasis on economics. First we had a long and detailed course on the economics of socialism. This was followed by an equally elaborate course on the economics of capitalism. The treatment of the subjects in this order had the fairly obvious purpose of filling our minds with a highly favourable picture of Socialist economics, on the basis of which it was not difficult to build up a strongly negative attitude to capitalism. The method of lecturing was dialectical. This way of arguing was ceaselessly drummed into our heads as the only valid method, and this produced for our instructors the rather disconcerting result that we began to use thesis, antithesis and synthesis, when arguing with our lecturers. This helped to keep bad marks off our records, since the means we used were 'correct', but we became adept at producing antithesis which, in turn, produced a synthesis that was well off the party-line.

We were encouraged to read international literature, and we were given the impression that although it was hoped that we would read 'progressive' authors, we were not to feel restricted in

73

our choice. We were, of course, restricted by the fact that we could not read books that weren't there.

Among the authors I recall who were recommended to us, there were:

English: Dickens, Jack Lindsay (Dickens was claimed to depict the English scene as it now was, if it was not worse, since a bourgeois society could only decline);

American: Walt Whitman, Jack London, Howard Fast (Fast has since defected from the Communist Party);

French: Emile Zola, Victor Hugo (these were tolerated as bourgeois reformers);

Russian: Gorki, Alexei Tolstoi, Fadeyev, and (selected) Ilya Ehrenburg. (Dostoevsky did not figure in the permitted list.)

The newspapers we read at the morning sessions included the British and American *Daily Workers*, the *Cominform Journal* (*For a lasting Peace, For a People's Democracy*), *China Reconstructs*, and the *Soviet Union Illustrated*, as well as the East German newspapers. Subscriptions to certain publications, including *Neues Deutschland*, were compulsory.

All this produced a considerable amount of double-thinking on the part of the students. We became habituated to falling in with correct Communist social and intellectual behaviour when we were in class, but among ourselves things were very different. Instead of arguing with our instructors about matters of fact or opinion, we allowed to grow up, when we were among ourselves, a strongly cynical and sceptical frame of mind.

Those who had no very strong intellectual grip learned what they were told parrot fashion and did not relate the conclusions that they were given to their experience of the real world. Students of this kind were not at all put out by seeing the glaring imperfections of the East German Republic, because their minds did not relate them to what they had been told in the classroom. Others of us did connect the two with bad effects on our progress as liberators of our oppressed compatriots.

We were also undermined as potential zealots by the growing feeling that a good many of the social science instructors did not really believe what they were saying to us. In later years quite a number of them, having survived by this form of intellectual prostitution, managed to escape to Western Germany, shedding their outer skin of red as they crossed the border. They were happy to have reached the West which they had spent so much time in describing as a hell on earth.

Among the other elements of our political and social instruction was the inculcation of atheism. According to our instructors, naturally, to believe in any form of religious idea was reactionary, illiterate and unprogressive. For practical reasons the Russians liked to give the impression that freedom of religion exists in their territories, but their opposition to it is ceaseless and absolute, and no believer can hope for political advancement or any sort of official job of any standing.

It was through these lectures that we were supposed to acquire a knowledge of how to think correctly about world affairs. Nigeria and other countries like it, on the way to independence, were to be dealt with in a very simple manner, like the Soviet Central Asian Republics where a large proportion of the population and virtually all the top party, government and industrial officials are Russians. This was what our East German instructors told us, but I doubt very much if the Russians themselves would have put the matter so crudely.

We did not learn, of course, that putting this policy into effect in the Soviet Union had involved great brutalities and had been strongly resisted by many of the nationalities now confined within the Soviet borders.

CHAPTER 11

Training for Subversion

Having been left in no doubt at the Bautzen school that it was our future to help spread Communism, Leninist theory applied only one really strict rule: that we should succeed and not fail. The range of the methods open to us was wide and too much scruple about method was not necessary. Admittedly this was not usually put to us in so many words since what was supposed to be our idealism was still being played upon.

At this time the Peace Campaign was in full swing and the Communist world was presented to us as the springboard of a noble plan to bring peace on earth. Only the Communists knew how to do this. Everybody else was either a ravening wolf or a misguided slave of the imperialists. We Africans, suppressed and oppressed by centuries of callous exploitation, could help in the fulfilment of this noble purpose. The Peace Campaign had its sincere believers, even among the students, but I do not think they were anything like a majority. There were too many inconsistencies. Indeed it was while I was in Bautzen that I had to undergo military training and it was in this context that the inconsistencies of the Peace Campaign showed themselves very clearly.

To explain the curiously liberal view that, for a time, was taken of student arguments about military training, it should be remembered that Stalin's death and the sense of release which followed it (however limited that proved to be) did ripple out at least as far as the edges of our little pool. Military training, even of a rather elementary sort, struck many of the students as incompatible with the Peace Campaign in spite of continuous propaganda alleging that the West Germans were re-arming with the assistance of the Anglo-Americans. It was, therefore, arranged that a demand for military training should be initiated by the students and trade union members. They asked for training to protect the Democratic Republic against saboteurs and spies who were supposed to be infiltrating from the West and to have recruited bourgeois remnants in Eastern Germany.

I was very soon involved in the training because I was an activist among the foreign students studying at the International Solidarity School. Only activists were to be trained from among those who belonged to the foreign students' group of the FDJ. The school itself was nominally controlled by the Ministry of the Interior in association with the Ministry of Education, but in practice major decisions, certainly the decision about military training, were made by the SSD.

I found myself one of a number of foreign students, shop-stewards, and clerical workers who were to be trained in the use of small arms under the organizational control of the local FDJ branch. We were a cross-section of young activists with a sprinkling of older men. The training school was near the Treasury building. No sooner did the plan for arms training begin to take form than debate began. It was the German students, rather than the foreign ones—we had been handpicked presumably—who pointed out that there was an inconsistency in organizing military training when the East German authorities were expending so much energy in presenting East Germany and the whole of the Communist world as devoted entirely to peace, in contrast with a militaristic West Germany which was alleged to be rebuilding the Wehrmacht under the guise of Hilfsarbeit.

I, myself, did not resist military training, but I knew from defectors from the West that this allegation was probably untrue and that all the West Germans had was a frontier force. Although the Germans who were naïve enough to take the Peace Campaign propaganda literally were firmly squashed in the end, the debate had a surprisingly long run. The doubters were told that they were gullible, and blind to the wickedness of the West. Defectors from the West could not be expected to know the true state of affairs, and their views deserved no respect.

It did not strike me as very odd then—although I admit it does now—that among the students and trade unionists there was a fairly deeply ingrained cynicism about Communist propaganda. We had the habit of listening with blank faces to what our instructors told us and to the party-line, but when we were alone we examined the propositions put to us on their merits in terms of fact. This was a very un-Stalinist thing to do, no doubt, but it meant that we were converting the method of the dialectic to our own uses. We did this even when we had no quarrel with certain objectives of Communism. In a way, I suppose, it was the sort of thing that students do anywhere in the world, but the issues had a sharper edge for us. Looking back it surprises me to remember that we used to make jokes about taking advantage of the military training and then ultimately using it to attack the Soviet Union.

The dissident Germans and ourselves, the Africans, accepted the military training on orders from above. There was a widespread feeling among the students that they wanted to have nothing to do with it. 'Ohne uns' was a sentiment that was strong, even among SED members. But later, people who declined or evaded military training were classed as reactionaries and were punished accordingly.

The first stage of our training was very elementary indeed. We went to a shooting gallery at the locomotive factory and fired air pistols at standard targets. This enabled us to be put into rough classifications. At this point I was the only African, and the only other foreign student was Grossman, an American Communist. After the initial grading the trainees were given progressively more elaborate instruction and we had to attend at first two, and later three, times a week. We were formed into platoons for drill and were given instruction in the use of small arms by an ex-army officer.

The whole organization was nominally part of the Sports Section of the FDJ and the army officer who instructed us in the use of the rifle and sub-machine gun was called the Sports Secretary. Our particular instructor, even during my time, eventually became quite openly an officer of the East German Army. I and my fellow students knew very well that the East Germans were rearming and that to pretend that military instruction was part of the so-called Sport and Technique Group was a pure fiction. Outside of student involvement in these things we knew that the Volkspolizei already included airmen. It was quite evident to us that there were far more policemen in Eastern Germany than were necessary for police duties. And we accepted that the defectors from the West were telling the truth when they told us that Eastern Germany was developing much bigger armed forces than

Western Germany. The attempt to conceal this internally in Eastern Germany was completely unsuccessful and was eventually abandoned. The police air school, for example, became quite openly an East German Military Air School. The trainees were given a new uniform undisguisedly military in type.

Our training was intensified when trade union trainees began to take a more active part. Rifles were issued and our instruction progressed to heavy machine-guns. Lectures and demonstrations were given in the dismantling and assembling of these weapons. We had intensive drills and, from time to time went out into the neighbouring countryside on route marches. We were issued with fatigue dress uniform. All this was done with Teutonic efficiency. We were tested from time to time and issued with a personal document in which the results were recorded.

I have no experience of military training other than this, but from what I have heard it seems to me that at this stage we were being trained in much the same way as any recruits would be in, for example, an OTC at a British university or in the early stages of conscript service. We were being trained to handle elementary weapons and to understand the words of command which enabled us to move in an orderly way. Nothing in the instruction suggested to us how this training might be used. That came later.

On our route marches our training developed to the extent that we took part in minor tactical exercises such as the use of cover, how to attack strong points in small groups and other similar movements. I did fairly well in this training but I must admit I sometimes found it arduous and disagreeable. I think that I accepted it partly because my day-to-day life lacked variety and partly because I was still convinced that my sheet anchor was success as a potential African leader in the fight against imperialism.

Anyway, when I went on to Dresden my certificate of progress stood me in good stead because I did not have to go through the elementary training all over again and found myself in the military training organization on a higher footing than my fellow students. The organization of military training was still nominally part of the Sport and Technique Group of the FDJ. In actual practice Communist control was exercised through the FDJ secretary who also held office in the SED.

Later in Dresden, as in Bautzen, I found myself in the midst of a students' controversy about the rights and wrongs of military training. In Dresden it was the Roman Catholic students, who, curiously enough, survived as a vocal group at this time, who made the running. They were able for a time to maintain a position of non co-operation. This they did rather cleverly by arguing, not on the basis of what their brand of religion demanded but on Communist propaganda itself. There were heated arguments, in which party functionaries, to their embarrassment, found themselves involved. But in the end the Catholic students had to conform or be expelled. This was the ultimate sanction which always enabled the party to win. Conform or cease to be a student. It was as simple as that, but at this period the party kept up a pretence of being gentle, and open to 'reason'.

Their pretences in other directions were very thin. Only a student who was nine-tenths blind could have failed to be aware that the so-called Light Machinery Factory was actually making aeroplane parts and training aeronautical engineers. There was also extensive training in flying gliders which anyone could see as they travelled about the countryside. When powered aeroplanes became available for our training, this enterprise was described as 'flugsport'.

I went to Dresden a good deal later than other Nigerians I knew and instead of being the only African undergoing military training, as I was in Bautzen, I was now one of a group. In Dresden military training became much more specialized and instruction much more technical. The instructors were actually members of the staff of the Dresden Military Academy but the authorities took the trouble to present them to us as mere technicians. The lectures were, however, genuinely technical, and relatively advanced. We had lectures on ballistics, the chemistry of explosives, and 'scientific' photography, which included the interpretation of camouflaged objects.

Some of the students took part in weekend training courses but I did not do so myself. For me the climax of my military training was the summer course which I attended at a barracks near Naumburg, in Saxony. This was attended by a great variety of people many of whom were foreigners, and there were many students from the universities all over East Germany. The barracks was a long-established one. It had been built in Kaiser Wilhelm's day and during the Hitler régime had been a school for air force officers. The complex of buildings, most of them long single-storey huts, was surrounded by barbed wire.

The courses lasted from four to six weeks and went on continuously throughout the summer months. The barbed wire, although it was not by any means impenetrable, served the double purpose of keeping off strangers and discouraging our excursions to neighbouring towns or villages. This discouragement was by no means wholly effective and most of the students were enterprising enough to get out when they felt disposed to do so.

The authorities, although they did not want us to be contaminated by the local population, did not seem to take our absences very seriously and no severe punishments were imposed. Indeed, our instructors made good use of our truancies. On one occasion there was a gala dance in the barracks to which girls from the neighbourhood were invited. Some of the trainees after the dance, which finished at the very proper hour of midnight, went off to the villages and did not get back to barracks until after 2 a.m. At a quarter to three the whole course was summoned on parade with full packs and taken off on a route march. We marched all the rest of the night, some of us feeling not quite up to it, to put it mildly, and our sufferings were made worse by having our steady marching interrupted by orders to take cover in the neighbouring countryside from imaginary low-flying aircraft, or to attack groups of houses or surround harmless, unoccupied copses. I found this very fatiguing indeed.

The training was arduous and efficient. We began by going over the lessons given on previous courses, but arms instruction now included detailed descriptions of weapons used by the imperialist West. Instruction and training was also given in partisan warfare. We listened to talks by instructors who had themselves taken part in guerilla warfare. Films were shown of Russian partisans in action behind the German lines during the Second World War. This was technically, at least, the moment when any remaining pretence that we were being trained to deal with saboteurs and spies disappeared. Moreover, this was military training, not sport, and we were left in no doubt, as foreign students, that the knowledge we were gaining was intended to be useful when we returned to our own countries.

In addition we were given political lectures which linked our technical training with actual or imaginable situations in which

Communists can properly engage in war. The lecturers took an orthodox Leninist line and we heard a good deal about 'just and unjust wars'.

After these lectures, it was the practice for trainees to form themselves into smaller groups to examine and interpret the implications of the formal lectures. We were directed as to the subjects for discussion and each group was led by one of the trainees or one of the instructors. It was during those discussions that the trainees began to speculate about the application of their training, against a background of Communist doctrine, to the situations in their own countries. Students from the Middle East or from countries in Africa dependent on Britain, France or Belgium, pursued the ideas which were chewed over at the discussion groups and carried them with them wherever they went. There was a kind of austerity about the whole business and a number of us began seriously to think about what we would do when we got back to our own countries.

The instructors did not by any means have it all their own way, for they were often wrong especially when they were trying to describe the student's own country.

At question time some of the instructors illustrated their arguments from their own experience or from the large body of legend about the heroes and heroines of the Russian and Chinese Revolutions. I may have been very innocent, but I remember being horrified by a tale, told by one of the lecturers as an illustration of noble devotion to the Communist cause, of a Chinese girl, beautiful and highly educated, and a devoted party member, who had been given the task of doing away with a non-Communist Chinese general during the Mao-Chiang conflict. So devoted to the cause was she that she became the general's concubine and bore him a child.

Somehow this story obsessed me. I found its implications disagreeable and intolerable. The story was intended to inspire us with admiration for the Communist system and its devotees, but it had quite the opposite effect on me. I could quite see that as someone who for years—this was in 1956—had been indoctrinated daily in Communist attitudes, it was remarkable that I should still be capable of being disconcerted by this commonplace Communist anecdote.

After this particular lecture I took myself off on a solitary walk to try to think the matter out. It amuses me now to recall that my behaviour on this occasion was noted by one of the instructors who must have seen me go off with a worried expression on my face. As I paced up and down he intercepted me. 'You do not look well,' he said. 'Have you a belly ache?'

The combination of technical training and political theory formed the theme of major lectures in the latter part of the course, which were given under the general title of 'Man and Technique in Warfare'. One question I particularly remember was about Nigeria. If it is the proper duty of a Nigerian Communist who has been trained in partisan warfare to make use of his knowledge and ability to further Communism in his country, how is he to get arms, since Nigeria has no common frontier with a Communist country? The answer was simple: it is the duty of a Nigerian Communist, who is a specialist in partisan warfare, to join the armed forces of the bourgeois régime in power and to try to destroy it from within.

I qualified as a basic instructor (*Gruppenführer*) on completion of the course at Naumburg.

CHAPTER 12

Charles and Anneliese

Charles Lucas was a full-blooded American negro from Chicago, whom I got to know intimately during my two years at Bautzen from 1953-55. Later in 1955, he gassed himself in Dresden; he was thirty-five years old and had been in Eastern Germany, a runaway from the American Armed Forces, for four years. He had fallen in love with a German girl he met in Western Germany. Charles's story was that it was on the girl's suggestion that they had decided to go to the Russian zone in Germany, believing that there would be no colour problem and that they could marry and live happily ever after.

Politics never really interested him, and the fact is that he had no very great capacity for understanding them. All he wanted was to be left alone—a forlorn hope in the circumstances. He was really neither anti- nor pro-Communist. Towards the end of my stay in Bautzen I was often in his flat and as far as I could make out his Bible was his most treasured possession. His Bible was in his hand when he was found dead in his gas-filled kitchen.

One of my Russian watchdogs, 'Colonel' Hubert, and Heinz Schattel, Direktor of the Bautzen school, often discussed Lucas. It was suggested at first that he might be useful as a bodyguard for me in some of my less popular duties. Apart from myself he was the only man of full-blooded African race there and, more to the point, as a protector, was an amateur boxer of some skill. At this time I had been reappointed by the school authorities ('elected' was the word used, but since I was the only candidate it was not to be taken literally) as First Secretary of the FDJ (Foreigners' Group). Charles had somehow—whether by design or accident it was hard to say—frustrated all the efforts of the Russians to show him off as a typical example of the American negro good enough to fight for his country—he had been a United States Army Sergeant—but unfit to be educated by his country.

My First Secretaryship, in which I had a certain amount of power of initiation, did not survive my attempt to escape to the West on April 21, 1954 (described in a previous chapter). When I returned from this escapade it was 'suggested' that I should resign the post but it was at the same time decided that I should hang on to my job as Organization Leader (Second Secretary) in the Factory Cell. The sacking was a rebuke, and my retention of the Second Secretaryship was an action of the 'collective' aimed at keeping me to the true path, and, of course, under direct observation, and without giving me much chance of independent action.

It was Heinz who said to me, rather solemnly and presumably by way of putting me in my place in the universe: 'You are very much mistaken if you think that through your defection you can upset our efforts to build a Socialist collective. While you have been running away, Lucas has been putting up a tremendous struggle for peace.' Lucas certainly wanted peace, but perhaps the kind he wanted was not the same as Heinz's.

One day, in Bautzen, I went round to Charles's flat, No. 4, Platz der Rotenarmee. Anneliese answered the bell. Anneliese's husband lived in the flat above and she herself shared her favours between Charles and her husband. At this time I had no more than the beginnings of a suspicion that she was a concealed party member and ssp informer. Charles was not at home. Anneliese asked me in and offered tea.

Her approach was hardly subtle and I decided to lead her on: 'Coloured people appeal to me because they are so warm-blooded', she began.

'But do not forget,' I countered, 'Charles is a boxer.'

'Ah, but you're no iceberg,' she replied, 'even two weeks with our wicked secret police can't have cooled your blood.'

'Well,' I said, 'I don't seem to be a warm-blooded fellow any longer—perhaps I have stayed too long in Europe. What I found wicked about the ssp was that they wouldn't let me have a smoke all the time I was locked up.'

At this point Charles came in with a bag of potatoes and onions. 'Hello, stranger,' said Charles. 'I heard you were back. Sorry if you've had to wait too long. I set out to buy a few potatoes, but

I had to hang about for nearly an hour in the queue just to see if they had any onions. It was Christmas when we last had the chance to buy any.'

Anneliese said it was about time she went and did some shopping herself, but before disappearing she seized the opportunity, presented by Charles's absence in the kitchen, to ask if she could come and visit me. I agreed. After she had gone I wanted to rush down after her on the pretence of getting some onions myself, but I realized that I had only about 3.70 marks (about six shillings) left. All the money found on me when arrested had been confiscated.

In his half German and half English, Lucas invited me to stay for eggs and potatoes, and he continued: 'Tomorrow I have to attend this preparatory agitation course for the atom bomb referendum.'

The party was whipping up support for the propaganda line opposing the foreshadowed presence of atomic weapons in Western Germany. Charles had his role to play in this, 'I suppose you're getting a good many chances these days to let off steam,' I said.

'That's just where I got nowhere,' he said, 'I was getting on fine, I thought, when the Class Leader told me that the group couldn't understand what the hell I was talking about. He told me it would be better if I wrote my piece down for the following Sunday.'

Lucas could write German even less than he could speak it. I asked him if he hadn't found the writing a bit laborious.

'Well, as a matter of fact I did write them an outline but it was thrown out. Unrealistic, they said. But I'm all right now. Herr Grundig, you know, our Marxist-Leninist tutor, has written a special piece for me to speak.'

'That's nice,' I said, 'having someone else do your work for you.'

'That's wrong, too,' said Charles. 'I've had to learn it and it's a good thing Anneliese had decided to shake off that Mexican buddy of hers, José, and pay a bit more attention to me. She's kept at me till I know the whole lot almost by heart. You know, these people are funny. They asked me to talk about my life in the United States Army and when I did, and I talked plenty, they told me I wasn't being "objective". According to them it couldn't

86

be objective that a coloured man in the United States Army had an automobile except it had been given to him as a bribe to keep him in the Army.'

'Grundig must know a lot about the conditions of American negroes,' I said. 'Six pages of close typing, not bad.'

'Christ knows where he got it from. I suppose all you educated characters get it all from books.'

Charles sighed. It was evidently all rather too much for him. His road to peace had a good many boulders on it. Then he said: 'Tell me, Ade, do you think people in Africa would give me and my girl friend a chance to live an ordinary life?'

I thought this one over and said, 'Surely they would, but you're not legally married, are you?'

I saw a trace of tears in Lucas's eyes.

'Yeah, I know,' he said, 'anyway she two-timed me because I couldn't buy her fur coats and take her to shows the way I could when I was with the Army.'

'But how are you going to get Anneliese away from her husband?'

'Who's talking about Anneliese? I'm talking about the girl that brought me here. She was educated. She went to school like you did. She's a very smart kid, but our happy home life packed up after four months. I was telling Grundig all about this. I asked him if there was any chance of me being sent to Africa on the job. But he told me the Nigerian Government prohibits marriage between blacks and whites.'

'That's news to me,' I said, 'there's no law that I know of that says that. Anyway there are plenty of mixed marriages where I come from, law or no law. But anyone who goes to Africa as a friend would be more than welcome.'

Charles and I talked a good deal, off and on, But somehow Anneliese always seemed to get in the way . . . .

It was July 1954. I had been 'rehabilitated' to some extent and the group were busy planning a summer vacation on the Baltic coast. Holiday places were, of course, fully planned in a planned society and there was no room for free enterprise in this particular sector. The holiday place was designated, accommodation was allocated. If you did not get a place there was no chance of slipping off for a private holiday of your own choice.

But we got as much enjoyment out of our planned holiday as possible. One day I found a letter waiting for me at 22 Karl Marx Strasse, unsigned, but with the code word 'Schultz II'. It was a curt summons to report the next day at the local party headquarters, which was in the same street as my digs. I knew from previous instructions that neither the school nor the factory authorities must know anything about my meeting with MVD or SSD but it was left to me to work out how to conceal the fact that these meetings took place.

Sometimes I pretended to be ill, but this time the notice was too short for that. With a certain amount of misgiving I decided to risk ignoring the summons. If asked about it later on I would simply say that the letter had reached me a day after the meeting was to have taken place.

Next day I followed my usual routine. The meeting was to have taken place at 3 p.m. I got back from school to my quarters at half-past five. I hadn't been in my room for five minutes when the bell rang. It was Anneliese.

'Hello, Ade, I have been doing some shopping but I thought I'd drop in for a few minutes' rest.'

I knew by now who Anneliese really was because on one of her earlier visits I had taken the liberty of going through her handbag while she went to the toilet. No wonder then that I was a little confused—and Anneliese saw it.

'Aren't you pleased to see me, Ade?' she said.

I made a quick recovery from my confusion: 'Of course I am, Anneliese. Please come in. You are always welcome—even if my room does look a mess with books lying all over the place. But what a pity that your visit will have to be a short one—in a few moments someone is coming to see me.'

I might have saved myself the trouble of trying to put her off. She went sailing past—right through to my bed-sitting room where she settled herself comfortably on the sofa. I was left with no doubt that her 'few minutes' was to last at least until supper-time.

'I might as well tell you', said Anneliese, 'that Charlie won't be coming with you to the Baltic because Schattel has just told me that I cannot travel with your group.'

'But', I replied, 'how can he stop you? After all, Charlie has already put your name forward.'

Anneliese, however, had a ready answer for this: 'As a matter of fact,' she said, 'I went to the trouble of seeing Schattel and a couple of other officials on this very question. They told me that the "vacation" was not so much a holiday as part of the school programme. What is more, all the students could go except those who were married—and that, of course, meant me.'

'But, surely, couldn't you have protested against a ruling of this kind?' I asked.

'I'm afraid it's final,' she replied, 'you of all people should know how stupid and pig-headed these Party Bonzes are. I don't care for Charlie all that much, but I know for a fact that quite a number of young girls always managed to get to the Baltic. It looks to me as though I've been written off as an old fogey. Perhaps I'm ready for an old people's home.'

'Well, you're youthful and good-looking,' I said. 'If you're an old has-been then I must be just about dead.'

'Never mind about what you think,' flashed back Anneliese. 'The party has had enough of me and seems to have thrown me over.' She spoke with a rasp in her voice. The bitterness and disillusion of her words was quite unmistakable.

Anneliese must have been on the verge of the thirties but she could easily have been taken for much younger. She wasn't very tall and she had a fancy for rather showy clothes when she could get them. She had dark brown hair, worn long. I found myself having to suppress my natural sympathy by reminding myself of her drab role on the fringes of the party. Perhaps I had made my own contributions to her miseries. I remembered this habit of hers of dropping in to see me every ten days or so. The party, whilst making use of her, obviously regarded her as expendable. They allowed it to be thought that she was rather backward politically. She mixed freely with foreigners, a thing that would not have been allowed to happen if she was not in a sense on duty.

This time when she visited me I was very conscious that I had dodged a meeting I was expected to attend. Was Anneliese after 'a few minutes' rest', or was she on one of Schattel's errands? Perhaps this time Anneliese really had come to relieve her feelings about her Baltic holiday.

All this atmosphere of suspicion and doubt about the people one met was characteristic of my life at this period. Nothing, no one, was ever simple or straightforward. Quite apart from the double role of individuals who were Communist activists of one sort or another, there was the mutual distrust between the Russians and the Germans to add to the general unease. The Russian Counter Intelligence had even taken the trouble at one point to put me on my guard against Anneliese, possibly because she was acting, in her inadequate way, on behalf of the Germans.

My contacts with the Russian Kommandatura, which was housed next door to the SSD, had made me familiar with the basic Communist classifications of the people they dealt with. People were trustworthy (in a political sense) or unreliable; intelligent (i.e. politically educable) or backward: some could be compromised by blackmail and there were others who were thought to have enough wits to present themselves convincingly as neutrals while really serving the party: and some were expendable or had to be 'liquidated'.

In those days I usually had a weekly discussion with a Soviet Army Major, a political officer whose function was *Komsomol* Secretary in the Soviet Forces stationed in Bautzen. Sometimes, however, either George or the Colonel—both of whom I met when I first arrived in East Germany—came along and took part in discussions on Soviet psychology or Communist sociology. George introduced me to the major as a friend who was going to teach me to play chess.

I got hold of all the books I could about chess and rather fancied my knowledge of theory. So I was rather taken aback to find myself check-mated within three moves by the classical Schafer movement. After several attempts I gave up chess. Major Nicolai improved the occasion by explaining to me that life and politics were like chess: when he deliberately offered me those pawns (in the Russian game they are called peasants), or threatened my queen, all his moves had the ultimate objective of check-mating my king. From chess we moved to life, from hypothetical cases to real persons, including, of course, the Germans, whom the Russians viewed, to say the least, objectively.

Shortly before my escape bid we had discussed Charles Lucas in George's presence and it was at this meeting that I was told that they had decided to drop Charles because Anneliese had failed to awaken his political conscience. I suggested that perhaps this was Anneliese's fault rather than Charles's. She was, after all, politically backward and had other disadvantages. But they obviously thought that political backwardness was not, perhaps, the ultimate test of usefulness.

The day after Anneliese came to my room to talk about the Baltic holiday, Frau Lehmann, who was Schattel's secretary, called me from the classroom to answer the telephone and I was told that the call was from a woman in the secondary school who wanted to speak to me. I spoke to her but all she wanted, it seemed was to establish my identity. Once this had been done I was passed on to Mani, the captain in the SSD. He told me that I should report at six o'clock the next morning in front of the 'Hotel Stadt Bautzen'. He added that it would be unnecessary for me to give an excuse to the school authorities.

When I arrived at the hotel next morning George drove up in his BMW and thus began my second association with the MVD. I could not have slept very well on the previous night because as soon as I had entered the car, I fell asleep. I could not have dozed off for more than four minutes because when I woke up and looked out of the car window I saw the 'Peace Bridge', the renamed bridge over the Spree on the Bautzen-Dresden road.

When we had gone over the bridge the car pulled up and we were joined by a Soviet Army officer who sat by the driver in the front seat. I knew I had seen him before, and then it dawned on me that he was the officer in charge of the house in Potsdam where I had been kept for five months, dressed in pyjamas. It was far from a pleasant sight to see this fellow, and once again I began wondering why I had been told to come to this unwelcome rendezvous. I decided, however, not to show any anxiety—bluff was obviously the best policy. Turning to George, who was sitting beside me, I pointed to the army officer and remarked: 'This comrade hasn't changed much except that he's grown a bit fatter. No doubt he's still at the same station.'

George looked at me coldly with an intense gaze that was rather frightening. Then he asked: 'Why did you keep me waiting on Tuesday and why did you not burn my letter?'

'Perhaps it shows I am no longer of any use to you,' I replied guardedly.

There was complete silence in the car for a few minutes and when George spoke again he was addressing the captain in Russian. The driver speeded up and we raced on till we reached the outskirts of Dresden. I felt in my bones that some highly unpleasant hours lay ahead of me. And yet, typical of the atmosphere in which I lived, they turned out to be quite agreeable. This was the carrot, not the stick. But I knew the stick was there.

Now and again, especially when we were showing dissatisfaction about something or other, our Russian 'uncles' would put in an appearance, always a source of inner questioning and alarm. They didn't bother, unless there was something to bother about, and they always appeared either without warning or made rather elaborate and mysterious arrangements, partly because it was their natural habit to do so and partly because they well knew that doing so put us in a suitably sensitive frame of mind.

This time, as we went along the conversation gradually became more amiable. I was asked how I was getting on, what I wanted to do, and what I thought about this and that. It was clear that they knew a good deal about how difficult and tiresome I had been but instead of threatening me with all sorts of troubles for my failure to keep on the party-line, they became expansive and jocular. And they took me to a very expensive restaurant and gave me a rich and splendid luncheon, well beyond my own financial reach and brought me back in the early evening to my lodgings in Bautzen.

CHAPTER 13

Trouble and Rehabilitation

In the middle of 1954, I had completed certain courses of instruction in the International Solidarity School in Bautzen. German language and mechanics were among them. But it was only in a manner of speaking that Bautzen was an academic institution. The Ministry of the Interior, the earthly power which was at this time in charge of my destinies, had a good deal more to do with the running of the school than the Ministry of Education. When a Ministry of the Interior representative appeared in the school, the Direktor, Herr Schattel, adopted very respectful attitudes and gave up his room and desk to the visitor. But even the Ministry of the Interior, on the principle of big fleas and little fleas, had to do the same thing for the SSD and they, in turn, for the Soviet MVD.

One of the carrots which had been dangled before me—indeed, it was the main carrot I was looking for myself—was the prospect of going to the University of Leipzig, and for this purpose I had taken, and what is more, passed, certain examinations. But month succeeded month without a summons to Leipzig. I probably made a considerable nuisance of myself to the Bautzen school authorities who tried to put me off by urging me to be patient, with one breath, and telling me, with the next, that it wasn't their fault but somebody else's.

I knew well, or anyway it was at the back of my mind, that my recent escapade in trying to rush off to Berlin without authority had surrounded me with a certain amount of suspicion about my basic loyalties. It was possible that the Leipzig plan would never come off, but I persisted, reasonably or unreasonably, in demanding action; and one day with the rather doubtful acquiescence of the Solidarity School I took myself off by train to Leipzig, determined to bang on somebody's table and demand what I considered to be my rights.

I sought out the *Ausländerinstitut* in Leipzig and demanded an interview with the *Direktor*. I did not get it. What I got was a long wait and firm marching orders back to Bautzen where I was advised to preserve my soul in patience, and await a summons when it pleased them to send it. When I got back to Bautzen, rather crestfallen I must admit, I decided to confront my situation as boldly as I could. Looking back on it I cannot help wondering what gave me this confidence, because I was powerless, and very nearly penniless. But somehow, at this period, my mind was very active and I seem to have had no hesitation in confronting authority.

I started off my campaign by showing that I was not prepared to have any further dealings with the Bautzen school. The control of the school locally rested with the Kreisrat. I decided to try to talk to Doktor Zieschank, chairman of the school's local management council, and managed to get myself, without too much difficulty, into his presence. Zieschank was sympathetic. He explained—and I could see this one coming—that he had no authority over students like us. The authority rested in Berlin, and it would be better for me to take up the matter of my future through the local party Headquarters. This I did, and with some effect, rather to my surprise.

I had had earlier dealings with State Secretary for the Interior, Hagen. Indeed, it was he who told me in May 1953, that I would be sent to Leipzig in September. This time Hagen had left the Ministry and it was his successor who had the files or perhaps was unwilling to find them.

I was summoned to meet the Berlin group in the Direktor's room in the school (Schattel was, of course, invisible). I was, apparently, to be given the soft treatment. Armchairs, cigarettes were provided in the Direktor's room. There were five visitors from Berlin including one woman, a Section Head in the Ministry. I recognized her from an earlier encounter. She was a young widow who had taken an interest in me while I was in Potsdam, but who now struck me as being someone who had thrust out of her life everything but the interests of the party. Strict and classical doctrine was her line. She sat at the desk with the paper and pencils.

I knew enough in those days to realize that the only way to get one's way, or to keep out of trouble, was to speak from the inside of the Communist mind. One tried to avoid showing negative attitudes or using negative phrases partly because it seemed to work better and partly because if things got rough afterwards or in some other contexts, one's negative views would reappear like accusing fingers.

Fantastically enough in this interview the jargon of our exchanges got itself off to a musical metaphor, and had difficulty in escaping from its toils. When I was told that Hagen was no longer in the Ministry I tried to indicate that I did not think this should necessarily mean that his decisions were forgotten or rescinded, or that there was no record of promises made to me. But the way I put it was to quote the composer Glinka that 'it was the people who made the music. The musicians merely arranged the orchestration.'

The widow attempted to crush me saying that 'the necessary criterion of good musicianship was the knowledge of the correct order of priorities which the notes should follow'.

If this was to be a game I could see no reason why I should not continue to play it. I observed that as far as I was concerned the decisive criterion was that of the time. It must confirm the correctness of the note order and the greatness of the musicians. By this I meant to indicate that I wanted to go to Leipzig then, and not later.

Our exchange of views lasted about an hour. My interviewers sounded to me as if they were both musicians and audience. The interview ended with my being told that my arguments had been academic and theoretical. I liked that, considering everything. I told them that I needed time to make up my mind. They told me that on the contrary, since their conclusion, on an infallible basis of Marxist logic was the only possible one for my positive development, there was no need for time and, presumably, nothing more to argue about.

They had an additional weapon in dealing with me because they knew I was running out of money. Since officially there is no such thing as unemployment in Eastern Germany, there is no unemployment benefit. I could either accept their terms or try to get out of the country—a dangerous action. It came to this, that I could either take a job in a local factory as part of my training with the possibility of blossoming into an activist in party cadre, or I could take part in the management of the school itself by helping to deal with new foreign students who might need a little guidance because of their lack of German. I was supposed to be able to supply this deficiency although the official reason I was at one time given for delaying my studies in Leipzig was that I did not know enough German.

I decided to take a factory job, and I am very glad now that I did, since it enabled me to learn more of the conditions of the German industrial workers and the methods used to keep them up to scratch and to exploit them as instruments of Communist propaganda, internally in East Germany and in the outside world.

I decided to work once again at the Bautzen locomotive works. After I had been on the factory floor for little more than three weeks the pattern of my future activities began to be revealed. I was, of course, sent to the factory as part of my political training as an agitator. The idea was that if I had direct knowledge of what went on in factories and of the conditions of the workers, I would be much more useful as an agitator than if I had to deal with these subjects at second hand or in an academic way.

This proved to be a mistaken calculation on the part of my 'managers' because it enabled me to know rather too much than too little and made me far from easy to convince in later years that the industrial worker in East Germany was so much better off than his 'starving' British counterparts. I got a good deal of insight too, by participation in the work of various bodies, into how men were 'made' and 'unmade' in the Communist sense.

It was, of course, typical of the Communist régime that a great many organizations were involved in the process of communizing industry. Not only was there a trade union system on the usual Communist model, but bound up with it all was the organization of workers' brigades, of one of which, of course, I became a member. There was also a branch of the FDJ with a full-time paid Secretariat and a branch of the SED and FDGB—the so-called Free German Trade Union Federation. All of these, with representatives of the management, formed the Factory Committee.

The ramifications were endless, and, from the various factory organizations, delegates were chosen to other bodies, up to county level.

The secretary of the factory's FDJ organization was also a county deputy, locally an important figure. He was Juri Heindrick, and I remember him telling me that he had signed an undertaking in Berlin not to marry, or form any domestic associations which would impair his mobility, for five years. It was Juri who outlined my future activities. This process began amiably enough by his inviting me to spend a weekend at his house. There I met, as if by chance, Captain Weber, who turned out to be already known to me, although in a rather limited way.

Abraham Weber was not yet forty, was bald-headed with little quick eyes which darted to and fro as if they were trying to jump out of his head, but which curiously contrasted with his deliberate, slow and carefully controlled movement of hands and body. He was not a man who was accustomed to being contradicted. The only man I ever saw him defer to in any way was Hubert, Ulbricht's personal secretary. Weber had a number of uniforms, a variety of roles and, very likely a variety of names. He used to appear from time to time in the Bautzen school, but he spoke only to the Direktor with never a word or apparently even a look to spare for such smaller fry as students. Weber belonged to the political section of the SSD but was, in reality, the representative in the local SSD of the Central Control Commission.

After this weekend meeting, Weber called on me in my one-room flat in Bautzen, and as a result of these meetings—or so I must suppose—I found myself a member of the FDJ Factory Committee and through that, by the usual process of delegation, a member of the local Bautzen FDJ Committee which itself was in direct contact with the godhead, i.e. the Zentralrat.

All these organizations were kept busy and in their higher echelons worked closely together. The Workers' Brigades were much concerned with maintaining and increasing output. The 'norms' were always being increased by Stakhanovite methods, and a good deal of resentment had been caused among the workers, whose general living conditions were by no means rosy in any case.

In addition to keeping the workers' noses to the grindstone and their minds well filled with praise of Communist accomplishments—the locomotives incidentally were all going to the Soviet Union as reparations—the employees were used as a source of propaganda. The workers were continually bombarded with anti-Western views. The RIAS and BBC broadcasts were particularly attacked presumably because they were, to some extent, effective. There were campaigns against religion and against certain rather absurd manifestations of interest in the West such as the wearing of Texan shirts. The Marxist theory of the inevitable absolute pauperization of industrial workers under capitalism was used in an attempt to diminish the number of workers from the East who were seeking a new life by crossing the frontier into Western Germany.

I well remember on one occasion that there was a meeting in the factory at a time when Holland was in difficulties because of the breakdown of its water defences caused by winter storms. The whistle blew. Work stopped. The factory hands were summoned in a great semi-circle round a speaker from one of the agitation groups. The Dutch sea defences had collapsed, we were told, because of the incurable inefficiency of capitalist maintenance. It was, therefore, the duty of workers in the Communist countries to show their solidarity with the down-trodden helots of the Netherlands by subscribing money to a relief fund and by passing a resolution condemning the Western capitalists.

This seemed to make a strong emotional appeal, and one of the workers from the factory floor vigorously interrupted the speaker and said that he would give a whole week's wages to the fund. The next two speakers made similar or more modest offers, followed by others of various dimensions. The speakers then invited support for resolutions, which was readily given. What I did not know then, but learned afterwards, was that these generous workers who started off the process of dedicating a week's wages were repaid in secret.

A good deal of our time was spent in attending lectures and taking part in seminars on the well-worn themes of the history of the Communist Party and the basic propositions of Marxism and Leninism. But the main task in which I found myself involved during this period was the build-up for the referendum on the subject of West German possession of atomic weapons.

In these days I had no spare time. The system made sure of that. In addition to my practical work for the various organizations I was studying, under direction, social science, with of course a strong doctrinal tinge, international politics, the fundamentals of logic and, by way of light relief, natural science.

The details of the referendum on German possession of atomic weapons has faded fairly quickly from human memory. It began, in fact, in Western Germany but was quickly picked up in the Eastern Republic. In the event the referendum was never put to the vote in Western Germany so that elaborate plans made in

Eastern Germany to send large numbers of young agitators west-
wards never came to anything. In Eastern Germany, however, I
found myself deeply involved in the system. Delegations were
formed from all the various organizations, and were to be trained
to go out among the voters on Polling Day. They were instructed
in the basic methods of agitation and were primed with arguments
which would enable them to make short work of any voter who
had the bad taste, or poor sense of self-preservation, either to
refrain from voting, or, if he did vote, vote the wrong way.

I went in charge of a group of about twenty youths all trained
to the eyebrows and supervised their excursions to villages in the
neighbourhood of our base. We had full lists of those entitled to
vote and it was our duty to tick off every name on the Electoral
Roll and to identify all those who had said they would not vote and
who proposed to enter a negative. The group worked hard on those
who refused to vote.

I remember in one village, there was a Protestant pastor who
was very stubborn indeed. Members of our group called on him at
his home, the village rectory. He was a middle-aged man with
something left of the authority which the Evangelical pastor once
enjoyed. His clothes were neat but threadbare and his house
showed evidence that there was little money to spare. Greeted by
the FDJ representatives whose task it was to ensure that he voted,
he took his stand on intellectual freedom.

'I am a man of God,' he argued, 'and there is surely no need for
me to demonstrate in this way that I am on the side of peace and
against the warmongers.'

The FDJ left it at that and reported the matter to the Centre.
The pastor's personal particulars were checked up and the arguments to be used, and the order in which they were to be presented,
were worked out in detail. A group of five were allocated to the
task of ensuring that he voted, and in the afternoon they called on
him again. When they knocked on his door they claimed the right
to enter and conduct the argument inside, which, in fact, they were
legally entitled to do. The pastor clearly did not like this but there
was nothing he could do; and his wife nervously joining in the
dialogue, was eventually dismissed by her husband, presumably in
the German manner, to the kitchen.

At first the argument was fairly gentle. The visitors appealed
on the basis of the general benefit of humanity to the pastor's

obligation not to stand aside from his duties as a citizen, from his duty to show in the community what he believed in private or from the dictates of his religious beliefs.

'But I need not do this. It is something everybody knows. In any case, surely, this is not like an election in which the citizen is choosing people to represent him. It is simply a case of adding one more vote to support a statement that is going to be made anyway, whether I vote or not.'

The pastor was stubborn. The second phase of the tactical exercise had to be brought into play.

'You must admit, Pastor,' a girl, who was one of the five, said, 'that it is impossible that it can be only coincidence that your arguments are the same as those which we know have been broadcast over the Western RIAS network, and further, we have reason to believe that you have not only listened to these broadcasts but have been supporting RIAS arguments in your conversations with the villagers.'

'But I have never listened to RIAS. I have no means of listening to it. I do not know their arguments. How could I have used them in conversation with the villagers?'

'You cannot expect us to believe that. You must have listened. We do not wish to make things difficult for you, but it is obvious that you are, by your attitude and your arguments, supporting Adenauer and the Western warmongers. We do not think that it would be possible for the authorities to continue to give you any assurance that it will be safe for you to continue as pastor in this village. The villagers all of whom have voted in the referendum will be too indignant to harbour a warmonger, a self-confessed warmonger, in their midst. Your cloth will be no protection.'

The pastor voted.

Yes, we worked very hard. The majority in support of the Communist view of the referendum was very large indeed; 96 per cent, I think. On the evening of Polling Day we were privileged to watch the counting of votes. I could not help seeing that some of the voting papers clearly marked as NOes were going into the AYE box. I had the temerity to draw a supervisor's attention to this.

In shocked tones he said, 'Surely you are not suggesting that a citizen of this loyal community would vote *intentionally* for Adenauer. It is obviously a mistake.'

And they were counted with the AYEs.

CHAPTER 14

External Affairs

My rehabilitation had made enough progress by the middle of 1955 for me to be fairly certain that I was destined for the Technische Hochschule in Dresden. Leipzig, for the time being, was still off.

During my last few months in Bautzen I was kept busy, too busy, as Second Secretary of the FDJ, looking after the school's ideological group. Considering my fatal ability to see two sides at least of every question, it was a curious position; but among the group I had acquired a reputation for being able to argue, and I could make rings round the simpler souls, or so it seemed to me, and so could keep my foothold on these dangerous slopes.

I was enrolled for the Dresden school in the autumn, and was going there with a fair wind because I had not only restored my credit but had even won medals. I was then capable of allowing my mind to work on two quite different propositions at the same time. I wanted to get away. Every way I looked I saw more and more the falsity of the Communist thesis, particularly as it applied to Eastern Germany. But I was prepared to work. To have done nothing would have been to destroy myself. And I was learning fast how to conceal my real feelings.

At Dresden I was to study what I can best translate as commercial engineering. Apparently painful experience had proved that to run a factory and keep the workers favourable to the régime, it was not enough to have factory directors who knew only dialectical materialism and the current party-line. They had also to know something about the technical side of the factory they were helping to manage. This startling discovery was to be put into practice in our case.

But before we went to Dresden we had to go on a practical course at the chemical works at Bohlen, where 12,000 workers were employed and where we foreign students had to show that we were fit mentally for the course we were to take at Dresden. I was a shining light of my group and had the privilege of living in Bohlen with the Second Secretary of the factory party organization. These things did not, of course, happen by accident, and I knew very well that I was thrown in with this man to ensure that any funny ideas I picked up on the factory floor could be corrected in the evenings I spent with him. I did learn a good deal about German doubts in Bohlen, and they helped to confirm my own.

When I knew I had to spend some time in a factory before going to Dresden I had tried to persuade the authorities in Bautzen that the best place for me to do my practical course would be in a factory in Berlin. But they would not have it—after my attempted escape.

The Bohlen course was good and I found a lot of it enjoyable. But in any case I was determined to prove that I was capable of taking in any instruction that was given me. I knew very well that the authorities were quite prepared to find any excuse to keep me from doing what I wanted if they decided that I was a doubtful political asset. But I was not going to give them the excuse that I was incapable of absorbing instruction.

We arrived in Dresden by December 1955, and were installed on the first floor of the Studenten Wohnheim, Block 2, in Guntzstrasse near the old Schloss Park (now the Peace Park). There was more in our placing than meets the eye. On that floor were the favoured foreign students, only two in a room. In the upper floors amenities were fewer; students were packed in six to a room. Visiting VIPs were taken to the first floor, and did not intrude on the others. We were paired off by order, and there was a careful calculation of partnerships. If one was weak on ideology, or showed signs of slipping into bad thinking of one sort or another, a partner, a *Betreuer* as he was called, was found who would restore the balance, or, more exactly, keep a good eye on what was going on inside one's head and outside it.

The Studenten-Wohnheim in Dresden was a show place, and we were privileged citizens in the classless society. But for some reason—accident of administration maybe—I had no *Betreuer* for my first five weeks in Dresden, and it was then that I began to make the contacts which were to have such remarkable results the following year, the year of the Hungarian revolution. Although I had grave doubts, I had at that time little direct experience of meeting young Germans outside the confines of the college or the FDJ.

My *Betreuer*, when he did arrive, proved to be an apparently fully indoctrinated German party member from Reichenberg. He was a real doctrinaire, who never allowed himself to be confused by permitting facts to come into his arguments. Or if the facts disagreed with his doctrine, he got rid of the facts. I think some of the brains behind our lives must have realized that the pure doctrinaires were not quite the right thing for foreign students. They seldom knew the real situation of the countries from which the foreign students came, but basing themselves on Communist doctrine, they laid down the law about these matters, often making ridiculous assertions that the students knew from direct experience to be untrue. Their whole proposition was undermined in this way.

The German-Soviet attempt to train students was, on the whole, unskilful at that time. This was because the relations between the Russians, more or less behind the scenes, and the Germans, were uneasy and full of distrust, or simply because so many of the Germans who got caught up in these processes were half-hearted, or, more likely, were waiting for the moment when they could discard their pretences and their Communism. That this was so was shown during the 1956 Hungarian rising.

The most remarkable of the students on the first floor at this time was Lim Hok, a Korean, who was in his fourth year of study in Germany. He had been a soldier and had come to Germany after the Korean War. He was a good deal older than any of us, and evidently led a different life when he was away from the hostel, which was often. He had connections with the Korean diplomatic representatives in Eastern Germany. He was the boss of the Korean group, and there was no doubt that he was a powerful figure. The other Koreans obviously held him in considerable awe. They were thoroughly afraid of him.

Lim Hok was a practical Communist, caring little for the doctrine but a great deal for discipline. He was supposed to be studying architecture, having failed to take to other subjects, and in any case his services were needed as *Betreuer* to a room-mate who was a German, and a good architect, and, to balance it all, a rather doubtful Communist with suspected religious beliefs, and Catholic beliefs at that.

At this time there was open war by the Communists against religious believers, especially Roman Catholics. Obviously there was no future in the Hochschule for a religious believer, and there were plenty of candidates for vacant places. But at this time, or at least at the earlier period of the epoch of which I am now speaking, the pressure on bourgeois elements had not yet reached its maximum, and doubtful characters like Gottfried, with his Catholic tendencies, and myself, with my ineradicable bourgeois background, were kept inside because, I suppose, we were more worth having than the *Dummköpfe* who accepted the party-line and Communist theory without question and were capable of understanding it no more than a parrot.

It was through Gottfried, and the acquaintances I made in the early, *Betreuer*-less, period of my stay in Dresden, that I got to know young Germans in unorganized social situations, and gathered from them, careful and non-committal though everything was, that there was 'another Germany' still, under the outward Communist society. These things were never discussed openly, but one could very often judge *by what was not said* that the Communist newspapers and other instruments of propaganda were not at all concerned with the truth, and that very many Germans—indeed it was pretty plain, most Germans—were merely trying to survive in the hope that they would still be alive when the whole period was over. I hope there are enough of them left now, but I wish I was as certain that the régime was coming to an end.

I went to parties, discreetly, and found myself in a different world from the watchful, suspicious world to which I had become accustomed. Nothing very special happened at these parties; no special revelations, no denunciations of the Communists or the Russians. But there was an atmosphere of simple friendship that made me realize with startling clarity the nature of the double world in which I had been living. I had been so long among those whose differences, if there were any, were within the context of Communism itself, that although in the past, in England as well as in Nigeria, I had lived in situations where opinion was unrestricted, I had ceased to be conscious of the contrast with my own predicament. These young Germans who were not particularly concerned about what I thought or did not think, and were only concerned to be themselves in a difficult set of circumstances, brought back to my mind things I had forgotten about ordinary human intercourse.

At that time it was sometimes possible to pay visits to Western Germany, always with permission of course. Even students went off to see relatives, and there was, one way or another, for Germans a remarkable freedom of movement. But as 1956 turned into 1957 things stiffened up, and it became increasingly difficult to make these journeys. I mention this not because I was a possible candidate for such a journey—I had no relatives in the West—but because it was part of a process visible in many contexts.

During 1956 a batch of youth leaders, including some of the foreign students, had made a visit to Hungary. Hungary had the reputation of having the best organized and most efficiently run Communist youth movement of all the Communist countries outside the USSR. It was held up as a model. And because of the relative weakness and lack of reliability of the German groups, authority considered that it would do some of them a lot of good to go and see a 'real' youth movement in operation. The whole affair is not without its ridiculous side, although it is easier to see that now than it was then. The German visitors to Hungary came back from their visit in a very curious state of mind. In their party there were, of course, fully indoctrinated members who made it their business to get their information to the party authorities as soon as the group returned: indeed had probably done so while they were still in Hungary. The Hungarian youth movement, instead of being a model for Communist trainees to emulate was a hotbed of sedition, seething with discontent, and about to boil over in violent expressions of detestation for the régime.

We often hear how efficient Communist organizations are. That is part of their propaganda on the scientific nature of their system. But in practice, the ordinary forms of human incompetence are commonplace. This was especially so in Eastern Europe, where the Communist régimes, though oppressive and powerful, had in no sense obtained the allegiance of the populations they controlled. One of the results was the almost farcical examples of inefficiency. If it had not been for the fact that these régimes had the power to punish their internal enemies in ways impossible in countries where the rule of law operates, some of these instances of inefficiency and incompetence would be thoroughly comic. But, unfortunately, laughing in the wrong place was a dangerous game.

Indeed, laughing at all was something we got out of practice at doing. We were, although we did not know it, on the verge of what, but for the ruthlessness of the Soviet Union, would have been revolution throughout Eastern Europe.

I have discovered since my return to my own country that people in the West supposed that it was difficult for people in the other satellites to know what was going on in Hungary. They supposed that during the uprising we had nothing to go on but the controlled radio. This was not so. We all knew perfectly well what was going on. In Bautzen, those of us who occasionally listened to non-Communist wireless stations did so furtively.

Now, in Dresden, pretence went by the board. We all listened, engrained Communists like the rest, especially to Vienna Radio. And during the Hungarian revolt it was possible to see hope rising in the Germans, hope that the nightmare might be coming to an end. There was fear, too, of course, fear of violence, fear for lost self-interest.

No one could help understanding what was going on. Party members always were members of various 'democratic' organizations which involved the wearing of badges. These began to disappear, or were worn on the inside of lapels. The students, as a general group, were excited. Some of them saw the great chance. They were prepared to take risks, possibly because they had less understanding than their seniors of the consequences of failure. Perhaps it was simply the optimism of youth that carried them on.

And what was the matter with me, an African? What concern of mine was it that some sorts of Europeans should dislike others? What did it matter to me if a few Hungarians got shot, or imprisoned for causing trouble? But somehow it did matter: and while I was finding myself more and more swept up in a fascinated interest in what was going on against Communist rule I realized that I, one of the 'bright boys' among the small Nigerian group in Dresden, could not agree with the majority of them about this or, it seemed, any other matter.

Students demonstrated, I with them. I wrote the text of a pamphlet, an anti-Russian, pro-Hungarian leaflet which was clandestinely distributed in Dresden by students. And the leaflet was printed on a press which was part of the equipment of the factory FDJ. It was a fantastic situation. The authorities found out that the leaflet had been printed on their own machines. They never found out who had written it, who printed it or who distributed it.

It is not for me to describe the course of the Hungarian revolution and its terrible consequences. So ineffective had been the training and indoctrination that I had undergone that I found myself, and not alone at that, wishing for success for the Hungarian revolution, and for a revolution in Eastern Germany too. There were students, right in the heart of a system that was intended to make them devoted Communists, ready to serve the cause loyally and well, who waited anxiously for the military intervention of the Western Powers which was to save all, even when the Soviet tanks were rolling into Hungary. It may seem hard to believe, but it was so.

Among the many lessons I learned, or hope I learned, was that the hard expressionless face of Communism hides misgivings and distrust. All over Germany students were trying to express themselves. In most universities and colleges something happened, sometimes great, sometimes small, which showed that the young people had not accepted Communism, indeed hated it. Perhaps things are different now. Perhaps they have become reconciled to their life under Moscow's domination. But I find it very hard to believe that they really have.

Among the Nigerian students in Dresden—there were about half a dozen of us—there were deep differences. We were being trained as a group, and it soon became known that we were to masquerade as the 'Nigerian Delegation' to the forthcoming youth festival in Moscow in 1957. Our mentors naturally hoped that we would learn to speak with one voice. But we didn't. Not by any means.

The main trouble, as far as I was concerned, had always been that the Communists, our instructors, based their arguments about Nigeria, and the dependent countries of Africa, on asserted facts which I knew were not facts at all. I was no defender of British rule, in fact I detested it, but it put me well off my stride to be required to accept accounts of what went on in Nigeria which were quite untrue. The British were a bunch of so and sos, and it was time they were kicked out of the place, but there wasn't a colour bar in the local hotels, and there was no law against mixed marriages, and the British administrators did not habitually, and by daily practice, ensure that their orders were carried out by the use of whip and club. The case against the British was strong enough. Why make it ridiculous by assertions of that kind?

Every time I came across statements of that sort—and they had a pretty wide range—I argued with my instructors. In fact, I must have been a very tiresome type of student all along the line. I was perpetually arguing, and disagreeing with almost everything that was said to me. By a curious perversion this seemed to increase my value. Ah, if we can really capture this fellow, he will be of real use to us in the future, they seemed to be saying.

My fellow Nigerians included some who understood very little of Communist theory, or felt it not worth their while to argue when obvious nonsense was talked. Some did not notice the nonsense, and some were stupid enough to think that the assertions must be true because the Communists said so. Their failure to see these things in Nigeria must have been due to their own blindness.

I mention these differences because they became more and more important as time went on, and in the end occupied our entire horizon. When the time came for us to go to Moscow, I had been transferred to Leipzig (at last), and the whole way from there to Berlin and from then on to Moscow and back we could do nothing but argue. The result was that we made a very unsatisfactory delegation, as I shall relate.

I went to Leipzig at the end of 1956. It had been decided, after a great deal of argument, that I should take a course in natural science. The Natural Science Faculty in Dresden was regarded as a nest of reactionaries, unsuitable for the nurture of such as I. At this time, the régime was still dependent on learned men from the pre-Communist period, and was forced to use them until such time as they had teachers of their own mould.

And I was in trouble as usual. Doubts were expressed about my ability to succeed in a natural science course. I was sent to Dr Leibnitz, head of the inorganic chemistry section of the science school in Leipzig. I joined his class, paid attention, and at the end of a short course was declared by the learned doctor to be fit for further instruction.

It was in Leipzig that the Nigeria group seriously began to be an entity. Before that there had been a West African group, but it never worked satisfactorily. Bowing to reactionary notions of national consciousness it was thought possible that if the Nigerians were put together they would work well, and the bright ones would influence the less bright, and the argumentative ones would be calmed down and made to toe the line in response to the appeal of national solidarity. It all sounded very well, but it didn't work. On the contrary, we knew too much about one another, and in the last resort arguments could become very personal, although that was not supposed to be the Communist way of settling disputes. It was in this group that the great ideological dispute blew up that was to occupy our minds to the exclusion of all else for the next few months.

CHAPTER 15

Festival in Moscow

The Sixth World Festival of Youth and Students took place in Moscow between July 28th and August 11, 1957. It was the first of the Communist festivals to be held in the Soviet Union and it brought delegates from more than a hundred countries—thirty thousand of them, to take part in a vast showpiece intended not only to impress the outside world but to show the Muscovites themselves the spreading influence of Communism throughout the world. Very large delegations came from China, from Britain and from Hungary, and from the smaller countries, particularly new States to which the Soviet Union was paying special attention, such as Ghana, there were large groups. Much was made of those delegations.

The festival included every imaginable form of activity, from ballet performances in the Bolshoi to lectures on 'the future of mankind', from football matches to film festivals, from exhibitions of paintings to tribal dances. The visitors were impressed by the sight of the great figures of the Soviet Union. President Voroshilov made the opening speech on July 28th at the Lenin Stadium where there also appeared in the central box such portentous figures as Zhukov, Bulganin, Khrushchev, Suslov and Shvernik.

Voroshilov, in his opening speech, struck the keynote. The festival was a festival of peace. 'Our great Socialist country,' he said, 'is engaged in peaceful creative endeavour . . . in the struggle for peace and mutual understanding you can fully rely on the Soviet people.'

It was into this feast of love and friendship that I and my fellow Nigerians came, filled, as far as I was concerned, with no sentiments of this sort. To describe how we got there I must go back to the situation in Leipzig.

When I arrived in Leipzig from Dresden I found myself in a

morass of dispute in which the West Africans were quarrelling among themselves, quarrelling with the management of the university, and with almost everybody else that came near them. As a newcomer I found that I was at some disadvantage because most of my compatriots had been there for some time and were more advanced in their studies than I was. Although this was annoying I soon found some compensation in my growing belief that if it came to an argument on Marxist-Leninist themes I was as good at it as anybody.

There were about a dozen Nigerians in the university who seemed to be solidly entrenched in the notion (in which they were encouraged by the local party) that membership of a formal student body (Landmannschaft) must be a condition of student-ship. This group had already had at least two years training in the Workers' and Peasants' Faculty at the university. I found myself from the very beginning out of sympathy with the group and attached myself at once to the only possible ally, Emmanuel, who, like me, came from Lagos. He and I lined up together and formed in effect a diversionary fraction within the Nigerian group. We were, however, cunning enough to conceal this under the guise of self-criticism and we began to argue from inside the group that the group itself had fallen into the grievous error of chauvinism, whereas we were true internationalists eager to cure the faults of the West Africans.

Controversy developed, and was helped by the lack of certainty among the local German intellectuals. It may seem fantastic, and I daresay it was, that we were allowed to spend so much time and energy in arguing among ourselves, but so it was. Among the issues we discussed, with great fervour and with a great show on both sides of wishing to be orthodox, were:

(i) The interpretation of current events in Nigeria and their future development. At this time the Communists knew compara-tively little about West Africa and their application of their pre-conceived notions had some very curious effects. We were expected to argue on the basis of alleged facts which we knew not to be facts at all. It was the classic contention of local pundits, for example, that slavery was used by the British in Nigeria and that Nigerians were excluded from vast areas of their own country, and, more trivially, that marriage between black and white was forbidden. There were many other false allegations—similar to those the Dresden instructors expected us to swallow. Some of the older group of Nigerians in Leipzig must have known as well as I that these contentions were untrue, but they were in a condition of mind—like some of my fellow Africans in Dresden— to accept the proposition that they had been blinded to the truth by living under a régime of colonial oppression.

(ii) The problem of the relations of West Africans in Germany with German women occupied many of our debates. We argued about the correctness or otherwise of formal marriage or other less binding arrangements. The German Communists who skirmished on the edges of this battlefield found themselves, it seemed to me very incorrectly, taking the side of the opponents of mixed marriage. Emmanuel and I argued that in doing so they reflected bourgeois morality and were in error, since they appeared to be worrying only about questions of social prejudice, which in our view a good Marxist would ignore.

(iii) There was much difference of opinion about the desirability and timing of industrialization in Nigeria. Our opponents thought that Nigeria should be industrialized at once and without consideration for what were to them such trivial matters as the existence of raw materials or even the beginnings of a supply of trained men.

I have mentioned these issues partly to show how we seemed to have spent a great deal of our spare time and partly to show how isolated we had become from real life. Our arguments had a wider importance, however, because one of the tasks of the Leipzig group was to be to choose new African recruits with the idea of forming a much larger, fully indoctrinated body of Nigerians who would, in due course, return home to promote the interests of Communism.

All these arguments made for bad blood among us and civil strife was in full swing when we were told to prepare ourselves to go to Moscow Youth Festival. We were told that all West African students were to converge in Berlin and that in Moscow we would have the dual role of forming part of national delegations and of approaching and assessing West Africans who came from the non-Communist world, as to their potential value as recruits.

Because of our attitude the majority group would have been

much happier if Emmanuel and I had been excluded from the Leipzig delegation, but we went with them despite strong efforts to have us classified as unsuitable. Our efforts had not been entirely unfruitful. A number of the majority group had swung in our direction. If we were skilful enough, we believed, we might even succeed in getting a majority, and at meetings which took place in Berlin we very nearly succeeded.

The night before we were due to go to Moscow there was a last and bitterly argued meeting at which we very nearly got away with it. We failed on the main doctrinal issues but on the resolution about our inclusion in the Moscow party we won by a a vote. Everyone was too exhausted to argue further.

The next morning we were in the special train for Moscow which carried the German youth delegates and in which part of a carriage was reserved for our group. The train went by way of Warsaw but skirted the city by branch lines. We were often held up for hours at a time and we got the impression that the Polish railway and customs officials were less co-operative than they might have been because of their dislike for the Germans. For Emmanuel and me the journey was socially uncomfortable because the rest of the party refused to have anything to do with us.

We took some pleasure in the fact that because Africans were objects of general curiosity to the other delegations we had no difficulty in making friends. As the train progressed into Soviet territory, there were many stops at stations where local delegations came to greet us. There was much speech making and flag-waving and enthusiasm grew as we got nearer the capital.

In Moscow the West African party was received by a group of six Russians, four girls and two men who escorted us by bus to the Hotel Yaroslavsky. There we found other African delegates who represented, or claimed to represent, Senegal, Dahomey and the Ivory Coast.

Now we were launched into the feverish activity of the festival. The local committees did their best to keep us fully occupied. Our daily programme was filled all the time with entertainments, lectures, seminars, parades. In practice this organization was so overloaded that it was continuously breaking down especially on timing. It is often said that Africans do not take time as seriously as Europeans do and that we tend to be rather vague about keeping appointments. We should have found the Russian approach to the same problem sympathetic. But whatever the cause it frequently happened during the festival that those who were supposed to go to X were swept off to Y, or missed appointments and did not go anywhere at all. I was all for isolationism anyway and did not get much pleasure out of excursions with the other members of the Nigeran delegation, in spite of the fact that we were now mixed up with other West Africans who had come from Britain and elsewhere.

One expedition I do remember was a bus trip to Yasnaya Polyana, the shrine of Tolstoy. On the way through a vast empty countryside, the bus broke down. The road had a poor surface and the cultivation of the fields which stretched endlessly on either side appeared primitive in comparison with what I had seen of agriculture in East Germany. Our escort in the bus was a Russian girl who told us that the nearest village was where she was born. It was necessary to go to the village to arrange for the bus to be repaired and I announced that I wanted to go too. There was some opposition to this proposal but it was not pressed and several of the party walked the couple of miles to the village with the girl. We were greeted with great kindness and hospitality by the villagers and saw the inside of some of their houses.

Nothing of more note than this occurred but some of the West Africans of the Leipzig group, particularly those who had always swallowed the Communist line without question, were clearly very surprised at what they saw. The contrasts between what they had been told of Soviet achievements and what they saw with their own eyes was very sharp. Their reaction was an example of what happens when reality, and no very terrible reality at that, is presented to people who had fully accepted the notion that Soviet socialism had perfected the human environment. This interested me because I knew that the Russians themselves did not make such lavish claims. It was their supporters who always went further than the facts warranted and exposed their converts to this reverse effect.

To the West Africans who were familiar with the very simple forms of agriculture practised in their own countries, the Russian village appeared as unmistakably and unarguably backward.

The atmosphere of Communist-run youth festivals is charged with enthusiasm and excitement. To many, quite possibly most, of the young men and women who come to these festivals from all over the world, especially those from countries which have been under foreign rule, however gentle, the Soviet Union has succeeded in presenting itself not only as a country where a desirable revolution has taken place, but where the new ideas which have accompanied that revolution have something to do with their own problems. The Communist propagandists have, in broad terms anyway, succeeded in persuading a great many young nationalists that the Russians are, in the long run, their only true friends, and that Western Powers, such as Britain, give up power over their dependencies only because historic forces, predictable by means of the dialectic, oblige them to do so. Their giving of independence is forced upon them and they try thereafter to retain power, by other means, mainly economic.

To young participants in the lively junketings of a Communist youth festival, the whole machinery of entertainment and propaganda is designed, and not at all stupidly designed, to confirm this view.

To see behind motives and intentions, it is necessary to know a good deal more than was available to the average visitor to the festival. Because of my personal history I did know enough to enable me to penetrate its façade. I had lived for years in an atmosphere of lies, distrust and barely concealed oppression. I knew what the average inhabitant of Eastern Germany felt about the Communist régime under which he lived. And I knew that the Festival of Youth and Students dedicated to peace and friendship was an instrument against Moscow's political opponents and not the feast of love that it claimed to be.

I do not know if the Nigerian group was typical of others. But it is quite possible that many of the other delegations were as much torn by internal quarrelling as we were. When we took part in parades, or put on a performance of not very well rehearsed and anthropologically very incorrect tribal dances, no doubt we gave an impression of a happy little band of oppressed colonials united in our dedication to peace and friendship and to the liberation of our people from the imperialists.

Because of our quarrel, and the deep suspicion with which I was regarded, I found myself quite often alone, or if not alone meeting visitors from various countries including a good many who had come 'for the trip' attracted by a cheap and enjoyable holiday in a place they would be unlikely to reach in any other circumstances. Some of these visitors indeed by no means found entertainment their only enjoyment; some of them attended lectures and seminars and argued very firmly against some of the pronouncements made.

I remember one Russian woman speaker on trade unions who tried to make her audiences' blood curdle by telling them with great dogmatism and a great array of apparently factual evidence, that slave labour was habitually used in the most brutal circumstances by the British in Nigeria. One of the Nigerians who had come to Moscow from London interrupted her and flatly denied what she was saying. This caused great embarrassment to the indoctrinated West Africans at the meeting who felt that this bold fellow was doing their reputation no good and obviously had no respect for the higher truth. The Nigerian who spoke was a genuine nationalist and as eager as anybody to bring about the end of foreign rule in his country. But he felt very strongly that the nationalist case was not assisted by being based on lies. This was a point that impressed me at the time because it reminded me that a great many of my troubles had originated on the same basis. I am not trying to claim that my conduct while in Eastern Germany was invariably based on a perfect regard for truth. I had got into the very devious habit of using the Communists' own dialectical methods to cloak my intentions, and the use of lies was a device without which one could not survive. But even in the period when I was trying my best to make myself an efficient and instructed Marxist-Leninist, I was often brought up with a jolt by the very false picture the Communists themselves had of some of the countries they hoped to influence.

But the Russians are quick learners. One of the lectures I attended during the Moscow festival was given by Professor I. I. Potekhin, now head of the African Research Institute in Moscow but who was, in 1957, Deputy Director of the Institute of Ethnography of the USSR Academy of Sciences. Potekhin has spent a lifetime as a specialist in African affairs. In 1932, for example, he was given the job of setting up a Department of African Studies at the Institute of Oriental Studies in Leningrad.

In my early days in East Germany translations of Potekhin's writings about West Africa were accessible to us and I was always struck by what seemed to me Potekhin's total failure to understand what made society 'tick' in the parts with which I was familiar. For example, he wrote about the society of Accra and of the Yoruba society of South-West Nigeria as if the whole momentum of the nationalist movement came from the urban proletariat and the peasants, a proposition I found completely unsound. Even allowing for the Marxist jargon with which Potekhin's writings were, at that time, filled, it was obvious to me that he quite simply did not know what he was talking about. However, this was the classic line at the time and during our indoctrination courses in East Germany I had more sense than to try to argue against him in terms of objective truth.

Ghana became independent in 1957, the year of the Moscow festival, and it was in October of that year that Potekhin went to Ghana on attachment to Achimota College for the purpose of social study. When he got back to Moscow in 1958 and began once more to write about Ghana, he wrote very differently and what he had learned by coming face to face with reality was very soon reflected in Communist political propaganda to West Africa. The Marxist jargon was still there but the society he described was recognizable. Behind the 'comprador bourgeoisie' I could recognize the West African businessman, and behind the 'intelligentsia' I could recognize some of the journalists and lawyers who had inspired the nationalist movements.

The more realistic approach to propaganda and political action which Potekhin's 'academic' studies in Ghana stimulated helped to make Communist penetration in West Africa more effective. This, of course, was unknown to me when I heard Potekhin's lecture at the festival. Then he spoke of the great role played by Africa in the struggle for peace and democracy. He spoke in Russian and his lecture was simultaneously translated into the major languages. He was very inspiring.

I attended a number of seminars which followed the lectures and I remember one in which we were invited to discuss the question 'Is the future predictable?' In the groups which discussed these large questions, there was always a leader skilled in the dialectic who gently and persuasively brought his often very mixed audience round to the conclusion that there was only one possible answer: that by means of the dialectical method and the experience of the Soviet Union and China, the future could infallibly be predicted, on Communist lines. This international seminar was also interesting because the organizers allowed a variety of opinions to be expressed publicly about the validity of Marxist prediction, and at the main sessions speakers condemned Marxist philosophy for basic weaknesses and also pointed out that a number of Marxist predictions had been falsified by events.

The seminar was led by Professor Oiserman of Moscow University. He stated the problem before the seminar thus: 'If the future can be scientifically predicted, it is then possible to envisage man's conscious activity in realizing aims planned in advance, and obtaining the results which are desired. If, on the other hand, the future cannot be predicted all rational activity of which the long-term outcome would be in accord with the initial aims, becomes impossible.' A good many of the people who attended the seminar firmly rejected the professor's view that Soviet philosophy was able to predict the future and the audience heard Marxism described as 'scholastic' and 'dogmatic' and 'grossly incorrect' in a number of its predictions. One of the Nigerians who came from London took part in the discussion. He was Kola Gbodi who declined to enter into the more complicated philosophical issues but was quite satisfied that in a general way the future could be predicted. Without foresight, he said, the struggle for the liberation of Africa would be inconceivable. Since it was possible to foresee the liberation of Africa, it followed, according to him, that it was possible to predict the development of society.

I tried to give myself a mixture of activities at the festival. A much sought after event was performances of the ballet at the Bolshoi Theatre. Tickets were issued to delegations and not to individuals and since there were well over thirty thousand delegates at the festival by no means all were able to go. I was lucky enough to get one of the two or three tickets given to our delegation, mainly as a result of the rather inefficient organization to which I referred earlier. I discovered a ticket in the hands of one of the delegation who, by great good fortune, had only the vaguest idea what the Bolshoi Theatre was and who in any case was lined up for two other events at the same time. While he was making up his mind the ticket was in my pocket. I also went to a concert at which David Oistrakh played and to a lecture by the composer Kabalevsky.

One of the highlights of the festival was a reception given by the Soviet Government but sponsored by the *Komsomol*, which took place in the Kremlin on the evening of August 5th. There was an enormous crowd which reports later said numbered about four thousand. There was a great deal of food and drink and speeches were made by representatives of delegations from the five continents. There was a concert by a Soviet youth orchestra. Among the members of the Soviet Government who attended were Khrushchev, Bulganin, Zhukov, Mikoyan, Madame Furtseva, Pervukhin, Kosygin.

It was a splendid occasion and the visitors were impressed by the splendour of the Kremlin and the sense of confident power which this international spectacle generated. But for us in the Nigerian delegation there was also a duty to perform. An African dance group had been formed before we left Eastern Germany and in the Lenin Stadium, under the floodlights, we gave a performance of African tribal dancing and music. We were all amateurs, and any connoisseur would have detected that it was not quite the real thing. But we made a great deal of noise and stamped about with tremendous fervour and agility. This went down well with the crowd.

But this was the least important of our activities. What we were really there for was to contact West Africans who had come to Moscow, mostly from London, with the assistance of the West African Students' Union, then under strong Left-wing influence. Because of my isolation from the rest of the group, I did not play a very effective part in this recruitment. But I did meet a number of the Nigerians who were attracted and, on the lines of the adverse opinion I had formed of the majority group, I was sure that the candidates were being picked for all the wrong reasons—tribal associations, personal relationships, family associations—and I made myself still more unpopular by saying so. Our delegation was supposed to be a group of fully indoctrinated Marxists, intellectually equipped to win any arguments that might arise with less enlightened Africans and be able to probe their characters enough to decide whether or not to recommend them to the German party functionaries. I did not think that many members of the delegation were up to their job.

When the festival ended we went back to Berlin by train. The returning trainload was quite different in composition because many young people from overseas who visited the festival had been invited to go to East European Communist countries on their way home.

It was from all this complex of contacting and influencing that the foreign students groups in East Germany and presumably elsewhere in Eastern Europe and in the Soviet Union itself, were changed and enlarged in the years that followed.

Emmanuel and I knew that when we got back to Berlin the old quarrel would be revived. When we got there the party offered us a Baltic holiday as a reward for our good work. Emmanuel and I declined partly because we had no liking for mass organized holidays and wanted to go elsewhere on our own, partly because the social atmosphere was anything but pleasant, but mostly because the holiday had to be paid for and we had no money.

So we went back to Leipzig determined to draw the attention of the authorities formally and firmly to what we saw as the fatal deficiencies of the Nigerian group. It was the beginning of my last, and losing, battle.

CHAPTER 16

Leipzig—Final Crisis

I cannot say that in the train taking Emmanuel and me back to Leipzig from Berlin I had any feeling of impending tragedy. I was angry and determined, and I was feeling all the complacent self-satisfaction of someone who has given up a pleasant experience —the Baltic holiday—to fulfil what I had convinced myself was a higher purpose. Anyway, I was heartily sick of the squabbling which had gone on for so long. I was also sure that we were right and they were wrong, and that provided a good deal of comfort in itself.

I realized that we were taking risks in isolating ourselves from the majority, and I wonder now that we had the nerve to go through with it. What we were determined to get across was that the other Africans were a poor lot who didn't know what they were doing and that they were bringing Communism and Africa into disrepute.

The essence of the dispute, leaving aside personal animosities and longer-standing issues, was: who is going to select and control the influx of recruits about to join the West African group, principally as a result of contacts made in Moscow?

When we got back to Leipzig we began to work out how we were going to put our scheme across. We were well aware, from hard experience, that it was no use simply to attack our opponents in a general objective way. Such a scheme would be thrown out at once, on the grounds that it had a bourgeois inspiration. What we did was to write a memorandum which treated the whole matter from inside. We presented ourselves as orthodox Communists who were distressed at the un-Socialist and deviationist attitude and practices of our fellow Africans. If they failed to exercise self-criticism we, more in sorrow than in anger, were obliged to do it for them.

The memorandum was prepared, copies were typed and were sent by registered post to the Central Committee of the SED, International Department, Berlin, where the key figure known to us was Peter Florin, and to the President of the FDGB (the so-called Free German Trade Union Federation) also in Berlin. A third copy was given, misguidedly as it turned out, to the Pro-Rector of Leipzig University.

The memorandum had four main points:

First: the Leipzig group had no real basis in Nigeria. It claimed to have a mandate from the Nigerian trade union movement, but this claim was entirely false since it derived from no more than a personal recommendation from a now discredited individual who had at one time held office in Nigeria. The claim that the Leipzig West Africans represented anything whatsoever in Nigeria could very easily be destroyed, and to found it thus on nothing was absurd and discreditable.

Second: not only was the group without any mandate from its country of origin, but the conduct of its members (apart from Emmanuel and myself) was thoroughly un-Socialist, making the group as a whole a cause of shame to progressive Nigerians and a danger to the future developments of socialism among Nigerians and in Nigeria itself.

Some examples: The group so gravely misunderstood the correct Socialist attitude to race relations that they had adopted the widespread practice of terminating by abortion pregnancies for which they were responsible involving women of non-Negro race. When new African recruits were being selected the group failed to exercise Socialist objectivity and therefore selected girl friends and relations regardless of the individual merits of those concerned as potential fighters for the liberation of oppressed peoples. The group opposed the correct views which had persistently and courageously been put forward by the writers of the memorandum, not because they did not recognize the force and validity of the criticisms but through fear of the consequences of admitting that they were on the wrong course. Their attitude was anti-Socialist, a fact revealed by their refusal to apply self-criticism. On a minor but potentially extremely mischievous issue they were gravely in error in that they sought to exclude from acceptance as recruits Africans whose faces bore tribal markings, their motive being the unacceptable one that Africans with tribal markings would betray their barbarism and bring discredit on the African representation. Tribal markings were inflicted on infants or adolescents and it was not in accordance with Socialist ideas to discriminate against them. Finally, the group were themselves guilty of tribalist attitudes. This was a grave offence which led to recruits being chosen because they belonged to the same tribe as those who selected them, without account being taken of their Socialist merits.

Third: the members of the majority group in many cases had the wrong attitude to education and were guilty of seeking qualifications as a means of personal advancement and not as a means of equipping themselves for the advancement of Socialism. They were guilty of careerism and opportunism. It was admitted that there were exceptions to this criticism since it was not necessarily un-Socialist for a student, for example, to give up the study of international affairs (i.e. Marxism-Leninism) in favour of medicine, since the right to practise as a doctor would enable a trainee returning to his own country to obtain employment by means of which he could advance the interests of socialism. But in general criticism could fairly be made against the majority group on this score.

Fourth: in view of the defects of the group as described in the memorandum, the conclusion was unavoidable that the majority representation must be formally condemned and prevented from controlling recruitment and future training of Africans. The true interests of socialism were understood by the signatories of the memorandum, who not only had the right as a minority to express themselves but, because of the obvious truth of their assertions, should be allowed to prevail. The majority group constituted a bad advertisement for the great international struggle for peace and the end of colonialist oppression.

We managed to complete and send off the memorandum while the rest of the Moscow party was still diverting itself on the shores of the Baltic.

The dispatch of the memorandum was followed by silence. The silence lasted for weeks. We were both alarmed and pleased about this. Silence could mean that the memorandum had been lost in transit and that we could pretend that it had never existed.

Or it could mean that the people to whom it was addressed had been so impressed by its arguments that our Moscow companions would never appear again.

While we grumbled nervously to one another the weeks passed. And then the reaction came. One day I received a message from Frau Schmidt of the Ministry of the Interior (at County level) in Leipzig telling me that no less a person than Ulbricht's secretary, Hubert, intended to come and see me and that it would be advisable for me to be at home to receive him. Hubert was not unkown to me. He appeared from time to time, sometimes sleek in civilian clothes and sometimes in uniform, although I was too unfamiliar with the differences to tell whether it was a soldier's or a commissar's uniform. Hubert and I had a long chat in which he spoke gently and reasonably. He said that the criticisms in our memorandum were well justified and that the authorities had been very much concerned about the behaviour of our group. But he appealed to me, in this tête-à-tête conversation, for forbearance. There were occasions, he said, even under socialism when it was not necessarily in the best interests of the party to tell the whole truth at once and to act on it.

'We have spent a good deal of money on these people over the years, and I am sure you will agree that it is too much to expect us to throw it all away without the fullest possible consideration of the effects. You must be well accustomed yourself to thinking deeply about these matters—your memorandum, of course, shows that you do—and it must be clear to you if you reflect for a moment that the party is wise to think in the long term. Even if only a very few of our recruits turn out well the expenditure is justified. But it would be rather embarrassing if we had to throw out the whole majority group from East Germany at one go. We might, by doing so, purge the ranks, but we would, on balance, suffer more than we would gain. The imperialists would certainly, for all their lack of skill, be able to exploit to our disadvantage the sudden appearance in the West of a relatively large number of West Africans.'

Hubert was frank and friendly. He asked me, in the interests of all and as a personal favour to Ulbricht, not to press the memorandum. It was tempting. But I decided not to agree.

Hubert also saw Emmanuel and, as I heard afterwards, talked to him in much the same way with this difference that Emmanuel's

German wife, who was certainly an SED member, helped to apply the pressure. Emmanuel and I survived this and the memorandum remained in existence like a rocket out of control.

I still find it difficult to explain why the authorities took the memorandum so seriously and gave us so much licence in dealing with it. Nothing would have been easier for them than to dispose of two unimportant and uninfluential Nigerians who had shown that they were not always ready to obey the party or to toe the party-line. We were a nuisance and since we were so argument-ative, very unlikely to be really useful instruments of Communist policies. I can only think that the issue was never serious enough for them to apply extremes. But I have a sneaking feeling that the truth is to be found in the opposite direction and that the Communists really thought that they were creating a powerful instrument of political influence in West Africa and that it was well worth while to play a long slow game in order to produce in the end a group of Africans who were satisfied with one another and whose mental processes were fully understood by their Communist sponsors.

In all the crazy and frustrating arguments and activities in which we were involved after the memorandum, ending in our both leaving Eastern Germany, defeated and, certainly in my case, completely disillusioned about Communism, I could never make up my mind whether the Communists were being clever or stupid about us. Looking back on it I think they were being more clever than stupid and that although they made many mistakes and did a lot of bad picking of recruits, they learned quickly by their mistakes. Perhaps in East Germany there were special difficulties, since the pattern of Communism was by no means indelibly stamped on the country or the people. We were fitted into an educational system which still contained a great many instructors who were, at best, half-hearted Communists or even anti-Com-munists who kept their mouths shut about their true views in order to eat.

Whatever the explanation may be, Emmanuel and I had a very rough time from the birth of the memorandum. But I doubt very much if our miseries were the result of a calculated campaign. I think they resulted from a mixture of premeditated moves and a great many entirely fortuitous actions which arose from fear, inefficiency, uncertainty or sheer indifference.

One of our own actions which contributed to the treatment to which we were subjected, was giving a third copy of the memorandum to the Pro-Rector of Leipzig University. I should have had enough sense to realize that the basic political attitudes of the university staff, however much they tried to disguise them, were very different from those of the dedicated SED functionaries and even more different from those of the Russians.

The Pro-Rector was on the whole a kindly man, who always gave us the impression that he would like to help. He did not regard the memorandum as anything very agreeable in the way of gifts. He gave us the impression that he could have got along quite nicely without it. His instinct, like a good toeing-the-line German bourgeois, was to pass it over to the right quarters, thereby showing that he was a good comrade who knew his duty and also a sensible man who knew when it was wise to refrain from dabbling in dangerous matters. He gave his copy to the Foreign Students' Welfare Officer in the university who was primarily an SED functionary. The Welfare Officer, in turn, perhaps on instructions or perhaps in haste to get rid of a hot coal, gave it to the majority group, our sworn and bitter enemies, and now back in Leipzig after their Baltic holiday. This brought matters to a head. Crisis had arrived. We were in the middle of a battle for survival. We, or they, must go.

From then until the shadows closed in on us, there was ceaseless movement. Bitter debate alternated with attempts at reconciliation and with efforts to make us abandon our attitude. The first attempts after Hubert's initial essay were made by the Ministry of Education. But they were the party men and not the academics, and had nothing new to say.

We never knew from day to day what the state of battle was and it was only by chance that we heard about a meeting of the West African students group, of which we were, of course, still members, called to discuss not so much our memorandum, but us, in our now manifest character as spanners in the works. We attended this meeting feeling, fortunately, just angry enough to ignore our isolation. We were denounced from all quarters. We were urged yet again to withdraw our memorandum. We were told that our views could not be other than absolutely wrong because we ourselves came from a bourgeois background. Even if our arguments were right, which was denied, no one could be expected to act on them because of our inherent defects.

If this had been merely an intellectual exercise, it would not have mattered so much. It might even have been rather funny. But from the meeting came the clearest of signals for us. We were confronted with the proposition that if our views prevailed, all the others would have to be expelled from East Germany. We could not be supposed seriously to expect the party to do this. We must, therefore accept the consequences of our refusal to withdraw the memorandum.

I am reluctant to give the impression that we either were or felt particularly brave in sticking to our attitude. I know that in my mind for a very long time had been the strong wish to get away from it all. It may be hindsight, but I had got to the stage when I was convinced that only by producing a crisis could I get away.

The critical meeting took place in November 1957, and its consequences soon became evident. I was summoned to the Pro-Rector's room. He regretted that it was his duty to tell me that if I continued in my refusal to withdraw the memorandum I could no longer expect to continue as a student in Leipzig University. This threat of expulsion had two aspects, both serious, the second more serious than the first. My studies had been very haphazard for a long time and expulsion from the classroom, although it destroyed what few remaining hopes I had of getting any qualification at Leipzig University, would have been bearable. What was much more serious was that expulsion carried with it the stoppage of the allowance on which I depended to live. The purpose of these threats was to induce Emmanuel and myself— for the same thing was happening to him, separately—to change our attitude and to allow ourselves to be re-absorbed, suitably contrite, in the West African group. Socialist legality was still in operation.

This period was an important one for the West African group because the new African recruits who had been picked up during and after the Moscow festival were begining to arrive in East Germany. Some of them came to Leipzig. The party management was either slack in its dealings with us or still cherished hopes that we might come round, because nothing was done to prevent our meeting those new recruits and attempting to convince them that we were right and that they should, on joining the West African group, take sides and vote for us. We thought that it was still possible for us to get our majority as we so nearly did on our way to Moscow earlier in the year. The party may have been open to conviction that a reversal of this kind would put the West African group on a better footing. I have no way of proving that this was in their minds, but I knew, and presumably the party knew, that among our opponents was a small number of clever, useful people and a larger number of mere yes-men or people too undeveloped mentally to understand even the elements of Communist doctrine. I may well be flattering Emmanuel and myself, but the party may have thought that our willingness to reach conclusions and our persistence, showed qualities of more potential value to the party than the loyalty of some of the more useless members of the group.

But it was not to work out that way. We were obviously contaminating the new recruits, and the position was becoming intolerable to everyone. Expulsion came in January 1958. The Pro-Rector gave Emmanuel and myself notice in writing (at least he signed the letter) that we could no longer stay at the university and that our allowances would immediately be cut in half. The next month they were to stop altogether.

When my allowance stopped I became entirely dependent on my wife's student allowance of 130 marks a month, a sum very far from enough to enable us to live. Our plight was made even worse by the fact that as a pampered foreign student I had been given good lodgings which had been furnished for us formally on a type of hire purchase agreement which involved deductions from my allowance of a sum said to cover the hire value of half the furniture. Gradually all our minor possessions were sold off. I even tried to sell the half of the furniture which I tried to argue properly belonged to me, but in this I did not succeed. We lived, my wife and child and myself, on the cheapest foods and in a state of wretchedness and worry. For weeks at a time I never went out, but now and again I made desperate efforts along with Emmanuel to get away.

Emmanuel and I had reacted to our expulsion from the university by saying: 'Very well, if we are not wanted, give us exit visas.' First we tried the Pro-Rector. He said he would be willing to help, but it soon became clear to us that he had no power to do so. All he could do was to refer the matter to the Ministry of the Interior. The only personal document I had was my internal passport. My Nigerian passport had been taken away from me in Potsdam when I first arrived there in 1952 and had never been returned to me.

Emmanuel and I persisted in our efforts to get visas. We visited every office we could think of. We stood in queues. We intercepted officials in the street. We haunted Security Police Headquarters. The police in fact seemed quite willing to be co-operative and for a time we had strong hopes that something would come of their efforts. But suddenly this stopped. Higher authority had been consulted and the police had been warned to 'lay off'.

The atmosphere in which I lived was nerve-racking and miserable and I was many times in complete despair. I wanted to leave the country, I wanted to get away forever from my surroundings and everybody in them. And more and more in the forefront of my mind was the feeling that I must get out to warn Nigeria of what was going on, of Communist plans to use students as instruments of subversion when they returned to their own country. I had been on a long weary journey up the wrong path and I could stand no more of it. But even then my despair sometimes took another form. My original intention when I left Nigeria had been to get an education, and I had still not succeeded in obtaining any useful qualification. It might still be possible. But even here my motives were mixed and when I asked for help to get me to the University of East Berlin, what I had in mind was that from there it would be easier to get out to the West. This came to nothing like all my other efforts.

I did get to Berlin on a brief escorted visit in April 1958, when I appeared before a commission to decide my future. For me this commission was nearly meaningless. I was too worn out to do more than maintain my demand either to be given an exit visa or to be sent to East Berlin University. The commission told me that they could do nothing for me unless I proved by my actions that I had given up my stubborn opposition to the advice I had been given in Leipzig. If I did this something might be arranged. Otherwise my case was hopeless. The only possibility that showed itself was that if I demonstrated a change of mind I might be allowed to go to Jena University. This did not meet my wishes at all. It was a move in the wrong direction, and when I learned that if I did go to Jena I would have to start on the most elementary level of studies of all, I told the commission that I would be an old man when I had completed the course, if I ever did. Back I went to Leipzig, my position unchanged and still without an exit visa.

Ironically, it was through my child's illness that I eventually got out of East Germany and back to Nigeria. By this time Emmanuel had gone. He was given a visa suddenly and without warning. When he got his visa he went with me to demand that I be given equal treatment, but this came to nothing. When Emmanuel soon afterwards left Leipzig, I learned that he had gone only by finding his flat empty when I went to visit him.

The combination of poor food and various domestic difficulties weakened us all and my child became ill with bronchitis. The doctor who attended us was friendly and helpful and produced a certificate saying that Leipzig was bad for the child's health. My wife's mother lived at that time in Potsdam and armed with this medical certificate I was able, at last, to have my internal passport amended to allow me to go to Potsdam with my wife and child. Whether this was a slip on the part of the authorities or not I was never able to find out, but I was now played out and clearly useless.

For me it was full circle. It was at Potsdam in 1952 that I had first come into the hands of the Russians and thence began my half dozen years as a potential member of Communism's advance guard in West Africa. I had been of no use to Communism and it had been of no use to me, except as a long hard school of disillusionment. Potsdam was a short train ride from Berlin and one day, alone, leaving everything behind me, I made the journey. It was quite simple. No one stopped me or even seemed to look at me. And I never went back.

I have not mentioned, until now, the fact that during my stay in Germany I married a German girl, and did not do so because the fact seemed to have no relevance to the main thread of my story. In any case, it is part of my private life, and in the outcome, a tragic part.

OUT INTO THE OPEN

CHAPTER 17

Return to the New Nigeria

In a way, everyone must be able to guess what my feelings were when I stepped out of the aircraft at Ikeja Airport, Lagos, after an absence of seven years. But I did not know that, at the time. I felt that this was something that had never happened to anyone. Not that that mattered: it had never happened to me, and that was enough to make it disturbing, even for me, I thought rather ruefully, despite my long practice in pretending to have one sort of feelings when I was, in fact, feeling something quite different. In a way it was rather like what one is supposed to feel on the point of drowning. I could scarcely be said to have rushed through in this moment my whole life's experience, but I did find myself making a quick review of my life before I left Nigeria.

I had grown suspicious of the glib things that people say about racial characteristics. They say, for instance, that the African's feeling for his family association is very strong and there have been moments during the past seven years when I had not exactly ceased to believe this but had stopped thinking about it except at rare intervals. But at this moment it flooded back into my mind with great strength. I suppose, not knowing what the future held for me—though I was full of zeal to warn my countrymen about the dangers that beset them—I was really clinging to the belief that there was security, and certainty and unrecriminating affection to be expected from my family. I was probably rather self-conscious about my situation and imagined that people were more curious about me than they really were. Before I left London I had been interviewed for one of the overseas services of the BBC and a rather one-sided story had appeared in a national daily newspaper.

Lagos took my arrival on the whole quite calmly. So did my father and my brothers and sisters. Outwardly at least. But to my father my return was clearly something of great importance about which he felt deeply. It is the Yoruba habit to celebrate with feasting and music all the major—and, it seems to some, all the minor—events which punctuate human life—birth, marriage and death, parting and homecoming, and the anniversaries of events in the real and in the spirit world. I was welcomed as my father's eldest son and my relations and dependants of my family were brought together to greet me. This was a lengthy business, because there is a proper way of doing these things, and in a society in which polite ceremonials play a great part, and in which memory of them is not kept fresh by reading books, exact repetition is important—and takes time.

But it took me some days to realize that I might as well give up any attempts to explain to my family, especially the older generation, the significance of my experience. To them the parts of Europe in which I had spent these years meant nothing, they created no images. And this was even more true of such airy and insubstantial matters as Communism and Moscow's plans for the subversion of Nigeria. I would have had more effect if I had talked about poisoned arrows being fired by the man in the moon. I had been away, and I had come back. I was my father's son and there was nothing more to be said.

A good deal more was said, of course, especially, I dare say, by me. One of the effects of living for so long in Europe was to develop in me a most un-Yoruba taste for privacy and silence, two things which were, to put it mildly, at a discount in Yoruba family life. I was not exactly treated as a prodigal son, but my father, although he did not pretend to understand my outlandish preferences, was generous in allowing me to reconstruct a part of one of his buildings as a flat with a sitting-room, a dining-room and a bedroom—with a bed up on legs—and a shower and other items of plumbing. I was touched by his kindness because it represented generosity plus an act of faith, since he did not require these things for himself. Nor, I think, did he actually hear, consciously, the pandemonium which afflicted me.

In Europe I had become fond of what is loosely called classical music. Despite the grip of Stalinist aesthetic theories on Europe, the Germans still contrived to enjoy their Beethoven, and one of the first things I installed in my flat in Lagos was a gramophone. But the moment the first strains of the Fifth Symphony came to my tired ears in the fourth-storey flat, they were drowned by other noises. One of my neighbours had a loud speaker known as a 'bulldog' which was louder, it seemed to me, than a massed band of Last Trumpets. Or someone had been born or someone had died or someone was being married, all occasions which called for drumming and singing and loud and ceaseless talk which came out of the neighbouring windows or arose from the multitude of little courtyards which lay between the closely packed buildings.

My father, whose hearing was acute, must have had some internal mechanism in his head which enabled him to hear selectively. I had no such device and I must have made a nuisance of myself by continuously complaining about what everybody else regarded as a natural phenomenon. It was, of course, my father's idea that I should begin at once to take an active part in the family business and I was encouraged to initiate a certain measure of modernization. I did so willingly, but all the time there pressed upon me the need to tell Nigerians what had happened to me and what it meant for them. I wanted to shout it from the rooftops. I wanted to hold meetings, to broadcast, to write for the newspapers. And it seemed to me that although a number of my old friends, and new acquaintances I made on my return, expressed a polite and mild interest in me as a traveller who had, perhaps, lighted on one or two unusual places during my wanderings I did not seem able to persuade people to grasp what I was driving at.

I would launch myself on a discourse about the possibilities in Nigeria of a 'popular front' government with Communist inspiration leading to eventual Communist control and all I would get would be: 'Yes, yes, my dear friend, but what do you think about the Action Group's prospects in the Northern Region in the next Federal Election?'

The Nigeria I came back to was very different from the country I had left in 1951. It looked different. While I had been away the whole tempo and power of the nationalist movement had changed. It seemed to me that the British, realizing—and indeed actually encouraging the process—that their best policy would be to bring independence much nearer than even the most lunatic optimists had imagined at the end of the war, had been rushing to patch up Nigeria into some semblance of a socially and economically viable entity. I suppose they argued that it was all very fine to encourage nationalist aspirations to their logical conclusion but that it

wouldn't do them much good if the whole thing collapsed five
minutes after it became independent.

There had been enormous progress during the years I had been
absent. That was evident all round me in Lagos. New housing,
new offices, huge port installations and all the rest of it growing up
around the old drainless, noisy, stinking slums of Lagos, which at
last were about to be cleared away. The British were still there in
the administration and in the technical departments. But with a
difference. It was the Nigerians' motor cars that were the big ones
now—except for the foreign businessman's or the foreign consul's
car which sometimes won by an inch or two—and the elected
Ministers were 'small boys' no more, but gave orders which their
British civil servants carried out, some shaking their heads in
gloomy prophecy, some shrugging their shoulders and wondering
where they were going to find a job after their inevitable resignation, and others devoted to the job they were doing, and to
Nigeria, and prepared to go on working in spite of the abuse and
the pain of their changed status.

As a good Nigerian nationalist, which by a somewhat round-
about route I hope I have come to be, I should probably be saying
'to hell with all those Europeans, especially the British. Devotion
to Nigeria is something that is reserved for Nigerians, like jobs in
the Civil Service. Maybe there will be a loss of efficiency, but I
think this has been exaggerated, too, judging from some of the
expatriates I see and hear in Lagos.' Gratitude, some wiseacre has
said, is not a factor in politics, and anybody with an ounce of per-
ception should be able to see that the Nigerians' natural instinct
would be to dislike most the people to whom they are continually
being told they owe the most. I had no particular dislike for the
British, but their 'mystery', of which I had been sharply if uncom-
prehendingly aware as a schoolboy in Lagos, was no longer
mysterious. They still had great aptitudes for being irritating. An
Englishman who may well never have had an imperialist thought in
his mind from the time he left his cradle, was quite capable of
making one feel that they still assumed that the black races were
intrinsically inferior. Perhaps such a person did not think this at
all, but he might very readily give the impression that he did
by merely, for example, quoting his house steward's opinion
about a local issue as a typical reflection of African attitudes.
I daresay if Danes or Dutchmen or Bulgarians or Poles were to

be in Nigeria in large numbers, they would show the same attitudes.

However, I felt it was no use the British complaining that they had done everything they possibly could to encourage Nigeria towards independence and to assist the country financially. The feeling of an African that he has been the victim of 'imperialism', however light the yoke, makes it impossible for him ever to rid himself of the feeling that had it not been for that imperialism, he would have been better off. Personally I do not agree with that view—it is irrational, but exists no less strongly because of that. In the making of emotional patterns of this kind, a little imperialism, a little mild foreign rule, is as bad as a great deal. This is all very unfair, but when were politics concerned with being fair?

I have come round from my early feelings of orthodox Communist antagonism to (always Western) imperialism to a position much less easy to define. What exasperates me chiefly about the British is that although they plod on doing the right thing in the most punctilious and polite manner, they do not show any sign that they really understand what is happening in West Africa. In a sense they do know, of course, but they seem to know what they know without any imagination and without producing any of the sparks which come when other less scrupulous and less, I suppose, well-informed inhabitants of the international political jungle, like Nasser and Khrushchev, have their say.

The British are in some ways too polite to survive in the rough world of West Africa, although nationalist sentiment favours the view that their nineteenth-century activities were brutal to a degree that would make Genghis Khan look like a scoutmaster. The mildness of British rule in West Africa has not given the British as much credit as they seem to think they deserve. The West African (if I can lump together a great variety of peoples with greatly differing attitudes) are now beginning to think in continental terms, and among the intellectuals imperialism, like peace, is regarded as indivisible. This means that if white men in the Union of South Africa treat Africans badly, and white men of another sort in the Central African Federation or in Kenya behave oppressively or cruelly, the white man in British West Africa behaves well, relatively, because the situation does not require him to behave badly. The white man in West Africa, so the argument goes, would behave badly if he needed to.

On the other hand, the British are so polite, and so fond of their cherished diplomatic language, that when one of them speaks out as the British Prime Minister, Mr Harold Macmillan, did against apartheid, a considerable sensation is caused—much greater than more forceful remarks from other types of person who are continually using abusive political language. Dealing with the British is rather like punching a very soft foam rubber mattress. You don't hurt your fist, and you don't do the mattress any harm, and the mattress quietly resumes its former shape. It is as if you hadn't punched it at all.

The attitude to Communism in Nigeria has been one of going too far in one sense and not far enough in another. Nigerian nationalists in the earlier days used to get a good deal of quiet fun out of telling the British administrators that they were nationalists and Communists. The administrators very likely had only a very dim idea of what Communism was themselves but they knew it was a bad thing and were alarmed to think that Nigerian nationalists were 'Reds' as well. But, in fact, they were not 'Reds' in the sense of being Marxists or people who lived in and through the dialectic.

Nationalists = revolutionaries = Communists. There was little more to it than that; something out of the oppositionist's dictionary. The administration some years after the war began to fuss about Communism and certain pronouncements were made. Specific publications were proscribed. The government announced that no Communists would be employed in government service. Newspapers were spoken to about the Communist menace, which had the effect of making a good many of the newspapermen laugh, and write about going up the railway track from Lagos to Ibadan looking for the Communists which they supposed must be hidden under the sleepers.

The fact is that Communism as a doctrine or as an organized body of men did not exist in Nigeria, in any significant sense. People there were who called themselves Communists and no doubt a number of students who returned from the UK came back with their heads full of half-digested Marxist language which very soon evaporated in the face of real life. Some young men who were carrying a well-lit torch for Moscow or the British Communist Party, were told by their fathers to put it out at once, and did so.

The Russians had a plan for West Africa, of course, but, even in Stalin's day, seemed to be content to spread the general notion that only the Communists were the real friends of the black races, that the Western Powers did not really mean to put into effect their promises of self-government and eventual independence. Once an imperialist always an imperialist, and imperialists are warmongers. This simple line had great influence and over the years must have made a large contribution to the neutralism which is sought after by most Nigerians, and I am sure by nearly all young Nigerians, no matter what their political leaders may say to the contrary.

Allegations about Communist wickedness were made for Nigerian ears by the British and Americans and discounted, or were inaudible over the loud noise of political axe-grinding which accompanied them. But when I came back to Nigeria, these days had gone. The Communists, as I knew from experience, had learned very rapidly about what was going on in West Africa. The days when they based their plans on the supposition that the industrial proletariat in Accra was going to dominate the West African scene had gone. Much of their enlightenment had come from the visit to Achimota of Professor I. I. Potekhin and his advice about who influenced what in real life in West Africa must have been invaluable to the Soviet planners.

While the British, and the West generally, give the impression that they pooh-pooh such infantile notions as pan-Africanism or Afro-Asian solidarity, the Communists are cashing in on them, having already a fair amount of credit from their easily won success in attracting Africans to neutralist ideas. The 'front' organizations, with the World Federation of Trade Unions, and the Afro-Asian Solidarity Committee in the van and the International Union of Students, the World Federation of Democratic Youth and the Women's International Democratic Federation whipping up the strays, are all, as I write, standing by for action or already have a toe, and in some cases, a whole foot in the camp.

There is no need for them to talk about Communism as such. Soviet accomplishments in such matters as Sputniks (the Nigerians are not interested in them mechanically but simply as proof of the USSR's progress) and in social improvement, even if that is only relative, are enough in themselves to attract. There is attraction too in the fact that Communism is a forbidden fruit. A young Nigerian who walks about the streets of Lagos with a big fat volume of, say, the *Works of Mao Tse-Tung* may well not read any of it but is expressing an attitude to authority by having it visibly in his possession.

And there is attraction for a country that is ceaselessly being reminded that it is under-developed, and backward, and that it will take years for it to have enough engineers to keep it going let alone progress, in precisely those aspects of so-called Stalinist methods that the West criticizes. African politicians are aware that in their countries there are vast masses of people who are illiterate and live in primitive conditions. Their natural endowment of intelligence is as good as anybody else's, but the only chance of developing their potentialities is to tell them what is good for them and make them do it.

When I think about this I remember all those endless lectures about the history of the Communist Party of the Soviet Union. I can even remember what my instructors in Bautzen and Leipzig would have preferred me not to know; I mean the battle of words, and more than words, about just what the vanguard of the workers was entitled to do, which was waged unsuccessfully by Trotsky with the feeble assistance of Zinoviev and Kamenev against the rising Stalin.

One could go on about this indefinitely. The Russians are obviously ready, with the achievement of independence, to move into West Africa. And the least that can be expected is a series of spectacular offers of economic aid which it would be asking a great deal to expect West Africans to turn down simply because they came from people of whom the British and Americans did not approve. After all, what harm have the Russians ever done to the Africans ? Where are the spectacular British offers of help ? I know that Britain has given a great deal to Nigeria and I believe will continue to do so. But she does it in her quiet smug way, carefully and slowly and without shouting it from the housetops. The housetops in Nigeria are fairly low so that they would not have to shout very loud to make themselves heard.

CHAPTER 18

Can We Survive Independence?

One of the characters who keeps turning up in West Africa is 'Uncle Tom', which means an African who admires the British, defers to them, believes that African nationalism has gone too far and too fast and that his country has got into the hands of a group of politicians who are not always representative of the best qualities of his countrymen. The 'Uncle Toms' think that the whole thing has been rather too much of a scramble and that when the British went, all sorts of latent antagonisms would be free to express themselves without the inhibitions imposed by even the light hand of British rule. God help us all, they say, in the hands of those incompetent upstarts. Some of the 'Uncle Toms' are able, intelligent men who keep out of politics 'because it is a dirty business' and spend their time either getting on with their private careers or wringing their hands. Such people point to Nkrumah as an awful warning. Although criticisms from such a source are sometimes valid, I believe these people are fundamentally wrong in their attitude.

Mr Macmillan's 'wind of change' was a fine phrase and made an addition to the contemporary vocabulary. But I wonder if he realized exactly where the wind was blowing and what changes it was bringing. I am sure that he would have liked to think that the wind, while it was bringing a number of new nations in the Lost Continent into existence, was also blowing away the old resentments and leaving a lot of nice new shiny African States, a little tired from their efforts, asking politely to be tucked up in bed with all the other members of the Commonwealth, all ready to turn when Father turned.

Real life does not strike me as being like that at all. The Africans do not embrace the Commonwealth association warmly like a brother. They acquiesce in it, somewhat sceptically, and largely because they feel that it would be rash to snub the Commonwealth in the early stages of independence because to do so might cut off welcome supplies of money and other aid. At heart many Africans—I would almost say most Africans—would like to do what Sekou Touré did to de Gaulle, but they see some material loss in the possibility that the Commonwealth and their American allies, might do what de Gaulle did to Sekou Touré. But even in this, some bolder spirits would at least emotionally prefer to shake off the association. Sekou Touré has managed to get hold of quite a lot of financial aid from the Russians and from Nkrumah after de Gaulle cut off his pocket money.

'Responsible African political leaders' do not take this line and I am quite ready to hope that their views will prevail. This does not prevent the next generation of Nigerians who are breathing down the necks of those now in power, skipping backwards a generation to the first fervour of nationalism and demanding what they call total freedom. Such people tend to see the Commonwealth association as another form of subservience or dependence although it is difficult to make them say what form this subservience takes. The impression one gets is that the politically conscious and educated Nigerian is possessed by a dream of a pure untrammelled African type of State which will be able to contribute something new to the world. This is a respectable enough aspiration as far as it goes. But I am unable to see the future in this way. The trouble with these young Nigerians is quite simply —and I am not being patronizing—that they do not know enough to judge these matters. It is not their fault. They have not been able to experience Communism for themselves. I have.

My conclusion, based on what I know of Communist methods, is that we Nigerians can maintain our independence, and our dignity as free men only by active co-operation (and this means a two-way traffic) between our government and the governments of countries that share our belief in our right to govern ourselves in our own way. I know that the Communist concept of independence, whatever their propaganda says about it, does not square with our own nationalist ideas. For a fully independent Nigeria to play a full role in the family of nations, we must remain uncompromising opponents of *all* forms of colonial exploitation. The average Nigerian is quite unaware of what happened to the nationalities now embraced in the USSR. He has never heard of the Lithuanians, the Latvians, the Estonians, and as for the Krim Tatars and the Chechens and the Ingushi, one might as well talk about the sad fate of nymphs and satyrs.

Some people have asked me whether my views presuppose the rejection of any form of external co-operation with either the Western democracies on the grounds that these countries still have in varying degrees colonial possessions or with the Eastern bloc on the grounds that its monolithic political structure is incompatible with African ideas of national independence. Nigeria, alone, would not survive. Indeed, no nation—and I don't exclude the United States or the Soviet Union—is big enough or rich enough to provide her citizens with all the necessities of life as they are judged today. I have heard all the theories about the differences between the right kind of nationalism (the Communist kind) and the wrong sort (everybody else's) but Nigeria is bound to depend in the critical period after independence on whether its inhabitants have a strong enough desire to be Nigerians and not Ibos, or Yorubas or Hausas—or 'homeless cosmopolitans' for that matter.

The test of international relationships is whether or not they can be entered into without any loss of national identity. Events on Communist China's border illustrate this point, but although Nigerians felt a very strong sympathy for Tibet when China finally over-ran it and although they are all on the side of India in her dispute with China over her northern frontiers, these places are too remote and their people too unimaginable for their fate at the hands of Communism to make an impression on any but a few.

Khrushchev seems to be distressed at the behaviour of his Chinese allies since it makes it difficult for him to present himself as a man of peace. But Khrushchev in the eyes of uncommitted nations has more to gain from this kind of embarrassment than by making sure that nothing divides his views from those of Mao Tse-Tung.

I certainly had my fill of the party-line and instruction in Marxism and Leninism, but I am often now rather glad I had to put up with it because it enables me to read between the lines of Communist statements.

In September 1959, Khrushchev told the Supreme Soviet in Moscow that practical considerations made it necessary for Communists to recognize the need for the co-existence of States in spite of differences in their political systems: at the same time, on the question of socialism (meaning, of course, the Communist form of that system) there could be no compromise. In other words, Khrushchev still follows Lenin in the view that Communism gives up temporarily its pursuit of world domination only when circumstances force it to do so.

The essential thing, I have come to think, is the many times repeated point that it is better, it conforms more truly with human nature, to live in a society which tolerates varying shades of opinion. This is more valuable than the material benefits which may conceivably arise ultimately and painfully in a society which ignores the individual. Communist theory and practice forbid feelings or actions which do not conform with Communism's mechanical view of the universe and man's place in it. Everything must yield to Communist conditions which, for their adherents, have the force of a higher law. The suppression of the national uprising in Hungary in 1956 seemed to surprise a lot of people. There was, in fact, nothing surprising in it.

Any Nigerian who wants to preserve his country's identity must reject association with Communism because it seeks, inevitably, to make an associate into a satellite. If we recognize this, we can still form the active alliances without which no nation can exist. Communists believe that much talk about freedom in the West is so much hot air. Their idea of freedom is that it is the recognition of necessity. I reject this interpretation.

My own belief is that in spite of the imperfections of the Western democracies—there are many—in most of these countries, public opinion has ultimate control over the governments' actions, including foreign relations. The British and the French have had to re-assess their policies to conform with reality. When I hear that the Soviet Union has granted independence to some of the peoples and to some of the formerly independent nations now under her rule, I may change my views. But not before.

CHAPTER 19

What Next?

Since I returned to Nigeria, my country has become a sovereign independent State. The yoke of colonialism, the shackles of imperialism, have been thrown off. Nigeria is a member of the United Nations, and is represented abroad by its own ambassadors.

October 1, 1960, was a great day. The British flag came down, and the green and white flag of Nigeria went up. The struggle of years had succeeded. The masters had gone. The great future of a great country, the biggest independent State in Africa ruled by Africans came into focus. Many simple Nigerians believed that independence meant that their wages would go up and that there would be no more sin. And some had never heard of it, and perhaps never would understand it.

But to all but the most backward of the Nigerian people independence meant something very real indeed, something tremendous and exciting and full of possibilities. And it meant this just as much to people who could see perfectly clearly that there was no automatic improvement in living conditions and that things might even in some ways get worse, who saw that the removal of the British hand on the steering wheel—it was little more than a finger at the end—might let loose all sorts of pressures that had been asleep.

I have heard head-shaking old Nigerians predict woe for us; and I have heard some old-fashioned or illiterate British say that they are horrified by the Nigerians' lack of appreciation for all that Britain has done for Nigeria. People who say these things can have no glimmering of understanding of what African or any other kind of new nationalism can mean. It is quite true that the modern concept of a State is not an African idea, and that Africans have, as yet, made little contribution to institutional or industrial life. But all that admitted, it cannot ever lead to the conclusion that independence should be withheld from people who want it, fit or unfit. And the Communists are right up to a point when they talk about the 'struggle' for independence, because it seems to be a fact of nature that there is less satisfaction from gaining freedom without a struggle than there is from getting it at the price of blood of martyrs.

Nigeria has its heroes, and very real ones they are. But fewer of them have been in prison, fewer have heard the sound of bullets, fewer have been exiled than in some territories which have won their freedom since the Second World War. But to say that does not in any way lessen the value of what they did. British rule, whatever may be said about Lugard conquering and ruling Nigeria with a handful of men, was firm and effective, and in spite of all the speeding up processes of the last few years, Britain did not give up power in Nigeria until it had to. It showed good sense that they realized that it was inevitable and that the processes towards freedom had to be accelerated. But it was Nigerians who made this plain. It was Nigerians who pressed and pressed until they got what they wanted. It is a thing that certain kinds of Europeans too readily forget: that in a man's heart, political freedom, whether it is in a material sense beneficial, or whether it exposes the possessor to dangers from which he was formerly protected, feels better than a position of servitude, however easy. The thing is obvious, and yet crocodile tears are still shed over the misguided wishes of the African who wants freedom, as they say, only to be worse off.

If only it could be realized that material benefit has very little to do with it, it would be possible to understand a great deal better why Jomo Kenyatta, and Hastings Banda, and Patrice Lumumba caught the allegiance of Africans. No amount of proof that these men have defects of character or intellect, that they are doing their people more harm than good has the slightest relevance in these matters.

But this said, I find it impossible to leave it there. I have had an experience that few of my countrymen have had, and I can see the characteristics and hopes and fears of my people in a mirror they do not know how to use. It is in this way that I find the present situation in Nigeria disturbing. So little is known of Communism, so little is believed about its methods and intentions, that most of West Africa is seriously exposed to Communist influence, especially the new, well-wrapped brand, which works through 'front' organizations, through offers of economic aid and through the presentation of the USSR and the Communist world generally as the Africans' only friend.

Anyone living in West Africa through the Congo crisis could have had no doubt about the effectiveness of the Communist line. It was so effective it scarcely had to be stated. Nor did Moscow have to do anything very positive. Talk was enough after their first unsuccessful incursion into the Congo with technicians and advisers. When they were thrown out, they were genuinely surprised. What had gone wrong with Marxist science? Someone must have turned over two pages at once. How could brutally suppressed Africans reject the hand of friendship of the world proletariat?

It was a lesson to Moscow, and one they were quick to learn. From that moment all they had to do was to stay at home and turn on the propaganda tap. The USSR is the friend of the true nationalist leaders of the Congo. Patrice Lumumba. The Western powers are against Lumumba. The USSR is the only true friend of African nationalism. Everyone else is its enemy. It was too easy, especially when it was made easier still by the monumental stupidity of the West and the criminal behaviour of the Belgians.

I found myself, in this issue, in a curious position. It sounds self-satisfied for me to say so, but I can put it in no other way than that the only people I could talk to seriously about the Congo crisis were those who knew something about Communism, and most of those were supporters of Communism. I was for Lumumba and against Kasavubu and Mobutu and Tsombe, by instinct as well as reason, because I felt that Lumumba was being attacked by the West for the wrong reasons and the others supported for the wrong, un-African reasons.

Because Lumumba was alleged to be a Communist, the West opposed him. They seemed to conclude that those of the Congolese who opposed Lumumba must be doing so for the right reasons and should themselves be supported. Even if Lumumba had serious Communist beliefs or associations—and there has been no proof of that—it seemed to me it would have been better to assimilate him than to reject him. And then Lumumba was executed, and became a hero and a martyr.

Some people seem to think that Communism is something you know about by instinct, in the same way as an animal knows how to swim. But it is not: and what I fear about my countrymen is that through sheer ignorance of its methods and intentions they will be unable to protect themselves against an influence they would not find of advantage to them in the long run. Communism needs study. But some Nigerians think that it is enough to study what the Communists say about their own actions and intentions in order to understand what is going on. But I learned the hard way that this is by no means enough for an understanding of the matter.

The West Africans are used to reading newspapers which argue with one another about motives, about events and about facts. The political parties dispute one another's points. It is difficult for Nigerians who have no special knowledge or experience to realize what it means to have every organ of opinion rigidly controlled by one party, by a State which does not tolerate the existence of an opposition. The Nigerians are an argumentative people. They would not take kindly to a society where certain subjects were excluded from argument because they were impermissible or treasonable.

It is not hard to see in what ways Communist propaganda is attractive to Africans. After all, they have seized many of the best bits of the polemical vocabulary. They are the 'anti-colonialists', they are the 'anti-imperialists'—always provided the colonialism and imperialism is not their own brand as practised in the Baltic States, or in Hungary, or in Tibet. The Communists back Afro-Asian solidarity, they back pan-Africanism from time to time, they encourage Egyptian and pan-Arabic hatred of Israel. They jump on every bandwaggon which will take them a yard further into Africa.

What many Africans do not realize is that many of the things which Communist propaganda supports are in fact anathema to the true Communist, and, when Communists get to power, they are rooted out. Nationalism is a serious fault, according to Communists. But one would never know that, African nationalists would never know that, if they listened only to Communist statements meant for their ears.

Africans have heard about Communism from opponents of Communism, notably the Americans and the British, and it is easy to understand why they listen sceptically. What makes Britain and America anti-Communist? Could it be fear? Could it simply be self-interest? It looks as if it might be both. Therefore, the Russians may prove to be our true friends. Let us find out for ourselves. After all they have never done us any harm. Why should they? And we need industrialization, we need a revolution in agriculture because our land is poor and needs large-scale intensive cultivation. Haven't the Russians and now the Chinese solved problems of this kind much more recently than the Western Powers? Is it not more than likely that they will approach our problems with more skill and sympathy than the 'imperialists'? So it runs.

But the Nigerians who believe these things cannot possibly know at what cost these things have been achieved, if indeed they have been achieved in the way the Communists would have us believe. How could they know about the millions of peasants who died in the process of collectivizing the land in the USSR in the 'twenties? Who remembers the seizure of Latvia, Estonia and Lithuania? Why, for that matter should the fate of such people matter. Europeans can destroy Europeans to their heart's content. Their record of brutality is pretty bad anyway. And surely Khrushchev has turned over a new leaf. He didn't have Malenkov shot, and Molotov is still alive. Not at all like the old days.

But they do not know that if Stalin is dead, Lenin, in a sense, is not. Communism's inner compulsion is to obtain power everywhere it can, and lies, and tricks, and the wearing of masks are still part of the technique. I am sure the African peoples will come to see it for themselves.

I hope they do not get hurt, all over again, in the process.